# Silk Weavers of Hill Tribe Laos

## Textiles, Tradition, and Well-Being

Joshua Hirschstein and Maren Beck
Photography by Joe Coca

Editor/Publisher: Linda Ligon
Associate Publisher: Karen Brock
Design: Michael Angelo Signorella



THRUMS
BOOKS
306 North Washington Avenue
Loveland, Colorado 80537
USA

Printed in china through Asia Pacific offset Ltd.
Library of Congress Control Number 2017933268

*This book is dedicated to our Moms:*

*Joy, for teaching Joshua how to see the world with an open heart, and*

*Ruth, for teaching Maren about color and textiles, and the value and beauty of things handmade.*


# Acknowledgements

We are deeply grateful to:

The many weavers, dyers, and other artists and families who have opened their homes to us over the years in Houaphan Province, predominantly in Xam Tai. They are the people writing the greater story. We are indebted to them for their expertise, patience, senses of humor, trust, and affection. We are particularly grateful to Sukkhavit, Lun and Bounkeo, Phout, and Souksakone; their friendships are our greatest reward.

Ms. Malaithong Bounyaxay, for her fluid translation skills, delicious meals, and warm friendship, and for opening so many doors for us in Houaphan Province. This book would not be possible without her efforts.

The Lao Tourism Office in Xam Neua, for consistent and exceptional service and support.

Mr. Khamsing Larddavong, Head of Information, Culture and Tourism of Houaphan Province

Mr. Phouvanh Phetmixay, Deputy of Information, Culture and Tourism of Houaphan Province

Mr. Khamphone Xaysavhan, Head of Tourism Division of Houaphan Province

All the helpful staff at the Lao Tourism Office.

A special thank you to our first guide and good friend, Mr. Kaiphet Thipphavong.

The regional Lao leadership for their hospitality:

Mr. Vhanxay Phengsomma, Governor of Houaphan Province

Mr. Hinthong Daunchansouk, Xam Tai District Governor

Mr. Phonechan Kathomphom, Xam Tai District Vice Governor

Mr. Maikham Phimmasone, Meung Kuan District Governor

Ms. Viengkham Nanthavongdouangsay, for her stories and support.

Zall Hirschstein, for the loom diagrams.

Marilyn Roberts, for helping us with the details of natural dyeing.

Carol Cassidy of Lao Textiles in Vientiane, for her assistance and support, and for her lifelong dedication to the silk weavers and traditional textile artistry of Laos.

Linda Ligon, for her support in a hundred ways. Her vision, passion, and effort are inspirational.

Joe Coca, for joining our venture and sharing his vision and cheer. May his rice fields always be green.

Finally, to Ari and Zall, for engaging with the adventure, having patience with their parents' idiosyncrasies, schlepping bags of textiles, telling their stories, and laughing (or at least rolling their eyes) when things turned weird.


*Authors' note:*

Lao to English transliterations are not formalized, and Lao words and names can be spelled any number of ways in English. Houaphanh may be Hua Phon; Xam Tai, Samtai. We have chosen certain spellings over others based on our research, ears, and, ultimately, because we had to.

We apologize for any errors or omissions, as this book's content is solely the responsibility of the authors.

# Contents


## one. Spark

CHAPTER ONE
Welcome to Xam Tai 6

CHAPTER TWO
Sukkhavit 22

CHAPTER THREE
The *Falang*, and How We Got Here 28

CHAPTER FOUR
Spark 35

## two. Setting

CHAPTER FIVE
Xam Tai District, Houaphan Province, Laos 42

CHAPTER SIX
Nang Tiip of Xam Tai 46

CHAPTER SEVEN
Political History of the Region 50

CHAPTER EIGHT
Yiim of Xam Tai 58

CHAPTER NINE
Entering the Twenty-First Century 60

CHAPTER TEN
Mai of Xam Tai 66

CHAPTER ELEVEN
Seeking Xam Tai's Ethno-Cultural Roots 68

CHAPTER TWELVE
Lun and Bounkeo 76

## three. Textiles in Village Life

CHAPTER THIRTEEN
Me Tau Lu of Ban Tao 82

CHAPTER FOURTEEN
Weaving as Well-Being 86

CHAPTER FIFTEEN
Sinh and Other Daily-Use Textiles 96

CHAPTER SIXTEEN
Ta of Meung Kuan 106

CHAPTER SEVENTEEN
Ceremonial Textiles 110

CHAPTER EIGHTEEN
Phout of Xam Tai 118

## four. Textile Creation


CHAPTER NINETEEN
The Art of Xam Tai Design and Motifs 126

CHAPTER TWENTY
Ban Tao Sushi 136

CHAPTER TWENTY-ONE
Silkworms and the Art of Sericulture 142

CHAPTER TWENTY-TWO
Reeling with Seuk of Ban Tao 146

CHAPTER TWENTY-THREE
Ni Mon of Xam Tai 150

CHAPTER TWENTY-FOUR
Souksakone of Xam Tai 152

CHAPTER TWENTY-FIVE
The Art of Natural Dyeing 158

CHAPTER TWENTY-SIX
The Art of Silk Weaving: Tools and Techniques 168

CHAPTER TWENTY-SEVEN
Template-Makers and Weavers 182

CHAPTER TWENTY-EIGHT
Chola of Xam Tai 188

CHAPTER TWENTY-NINE
Cotton Textiles 192

CHAPTER THIRTY
Dyeing with Indigo 196


## five. Looking Forward


CHAPTER THIRTY-ONE
The Marketplace 202

CHAPTER THIRTY-TWO
Mai of Meung Kuan 206

CHAPTER THIRTY-THREE
The Dance of the Young Weavers 208

CHAPTER THIRTY-FOUR
Mai Chom of Xam Tai 212

EPILOGUE
The Final Word 214

Bibliography and Photography Credits 216

Index 217

# one. Spark

*Each of us has a spark of life inside us,*
*and our highest endeavor ought to be*
*to set off that spark in one another.*

—Kenny Ausubel

CHAPTER ONE

# Welcome to Xam Tai

TWO SMALL BOYS, one naked and one wearing only a tee shirt, ran blindly towards us, laughing. They each held a stick and they were taking turns whapping a bicycle tire rim to continue it on its bumpy path. Looking up from their game, they saw us four *falang*—Maren, me and our twelve- and nine-year-old sons, Ari and Zall—and they both stopped mid-stride. The tire rim itself rolled forward another twenty feet, directly into Maren's outstretched hand. She smiled: "Sabaidee," she greeted.

The two little boys stood still for a moment, and then one turned and fled back to safety. The other stood wide-eyed, frozen. An older boy, dressed for school in a white shirt and

Opposite: The main road as it climbs over the hill into Xam Tai village. Above: A sign directing people to the Xam Tai's Provincial Office of Transportation; behind is the local soccer field, which is adjacent to the district's middle and secondary schools.

A traditional house in Xam Tai village provides a gathering place for neighbors.

dark pants, now saw us as well and shouted something that thawed the toddler. The little boy looked back at the shouter, then at us, then turned and ran in the direction of his original playmate.

The older boy, wearing a broad smile, trotted towards us; before he had reached our side, he blurted out as one long word: "Hellowhatisyourname?"

"My name is Maren," enunciated Maren slowly. "What is your name?"

"Ma-ren," he repeated, then: "MynameisBoun. Gladtomeetyou." He turned to Ari, extended a hand, and repeated: "Hellowhatisyourname?"

Before Ari could answer, another boy came running up shouting "Hellowhatisyourname?" Ari pronounced his name for both, and then each boy asked Zall his name. Zall's "z" sound proved a challenge and the boys smiled as they tried to turn a buzzing "zhhhh" into a delicate "zzzz." We all laughed at the beehive sounds.

Two more children joined. Everyone wanted a turn with "Hello what is your name?" and we were finally rescued from the lengthy introductions when a woman emerged from the nearest home tightening her *sinh* around her waist.

"Sabaidee," Maren nodded towards the woman, pressing her hands quickly together under her chin in the traditional greeting.

Youthful energy is abundant.

"Sabaidee," the women returned with a bright smile and a casual bow and hand press. She pointed to our two blond boys and said something that made the gathered children laugh.

Our guide and translator, Kaiphet, quickly stepped up from behind, introduced us, and inquired as to whether there were any weavers in the village. We had read in travel books about the traditional silk and cotton weaving of Laos's Houaphan Province, and we had seen samples of the quality weaving in Laos's major hub, Luang Prabang. We had also seen glimpses of looms under many homes as we had approached Xam Tai on the bus.

The woman nodded and pointed to a bench in the shade under her home. With a wave of her hand, she invited us to sit on the smooth-worn benches; we waited patiently as Kaiphet and the woman exchanged what we assumed were pleasantries. To our left rested a dusty wooden plow and a stack of aged, cracked hardwood boards. On the right were several wide, handwoven baskets, each covered with a section of decaying brown tarp.

We had arrived in Xam Tai, in the southern section of Houaphan Province in northeast Laos, at 3 pm after a seven-hour bus ride from Xam Neua over the twisty jungle mountains. We had deposited our packs in a cement box of a room in the

Below: A young girl peers out from the upstairs window.
Right: A weaver in Xam Tai works in the cool shade of her home.

town's sole guesthouse, and—what else to do?—walked the half hour beyond the central market and the bus station, past where the paved lane ended. The rutted dirt road, far more suited for the motorcycle than the rare four-wheel-drive vehicle, tumbled over a hillock and brought us to old Xam Tai's several dozen homes. One main road cut down the neighborhood's center; raised-stilt homes, a few with thatched roofs but most with metal, lined both sides. More homes straddled a thin, rutted lane behind the front row of houses.

Surrounding us were dusty browns and tans, from the houses' aged wooden posts to the unfinished crude boards of the houses' siding to the thick, dry roof thatch. A band of the forest's deep jungle green edged the periphery. The sky was hazy blue.

The woman stood up, readjusted her faded cotton sinh, and beckoned us to join her around behind the stack of lumber to what looked like a four-post canopy bed; she shooed a couple chickens off a worn, stained sheet that covered the structure and pulled off the dust cover.

The complex four-posted loom apparatus was strung with a dizzying, seemingly chaotic array of tan string, pink plastic ties, and smooth-worn sticks. The extended warp, which wrapped across, up, and over the loom, glowed with rich red. A glimmer of supplemental color—a bit of purple and yellow—danced a hint of expression on the front bar of the loom; the rest of the

The "back alley" of Xam Tai village; looms are set up under virtually every home.

A weaver hand-picks the supplemental colors into her textile. The recent advent of reliable electricity, and thus the light bulb, has substantially increased the time a weaver can spend at her loom.

completed textile was hidden, as it had been rolled tightly during the weaving process with the bottomside up onto the loom's rolling front bar.

The woman disconnected the front bar and delicately unrolled the completed three-foot section, making sure not to create excess tension on the still-connected warp threads. With a smile she backed up so we could see the textile she had in progress.

The silk shimmered like a jewel—a burst of opulence and intricacy and precision in reds and yellows and purples that reached deep and sure. The bold Escheresque geometric design—Was this an elephant? Was this a man standing? Was this the rice awaiting harvest?—defied the "simpleness" of our surroundings.

We looked closer. A thousand—no, a hundred thousand—threads of spirited color have been cajoled and tamed into a woven dance of the exquisite and refined.

"Please, show us how?" Maren asked in English. No translation was needed.

The woman sat down on the worn bench, re-rolled the textile onto the bar, adjusted a plastic tie attached to the comb, lifted a wide set of threads with a wooden weaver's sword, and passed her hand-smoothed shuttle between the threads, adding another line of red weft. We sat mesmerized for several minutes, watching her pass the shuttle across the warp, and then hand-pick a selection of bright silk threads across each row.

Two more women who must have heard

Maren's "oohs and aahs" appeared on the porch above and leaned over the narrow wooden railing. We looked up and smiled. "Sabaidee."

"Sabaidee-ee," they smiled back, holding the last long-e tone an extra beat. One of them said something and the weaver broke into a bright grin. The weaver didn't miss a beat, continuing to work her hands, methodically picking the discontinuous supplemental pattern threads into the textile's exposed backside. Three young, bottom-naked children appeared from the home and clung to the two women's knees, staring down at us from the overhead porch.

Ari, our twelve-year-old son, offered them a wide grin; the three little boys stared. One pointed and said "Falang." The other little boys quickly repeated: "Falang, falang!" Ari nodded at their welcome, which literally means "French," but today refers to any westerner. Zall, our nine-year-old, raised his ever-present Nikon and snapped a shot of the boys clinging to their mothers' legs.

Maren leaned down close to the woman's loom to study its intricacies. The weaver kept working, knowing she was being studied. Two more children, perhaps nine- or ten-year-olds in grubby tee shirts, sagging shorts, and flip-flops, ran over to join the growing crowd, bringing with them a dog and a whirl of dust. A chicken with a fleet of chicks scurried by our feet and ran out of the cool of the home's shade.

"What is she weaving?" we ask Kaiphet. Kaiphet translated the sentence into Lao and received a three-sentence reply, and

A weaver takes a break from her concentration at her loom.

Weavers patiently take turns showing us their textiles.

then turned to us.

"She say it is for a...uh...ceremony," translated Kaiphet. His brow crinkled as he searched for the best words. "It is *phaa sabai*, but, uh, I do not know how to say in English—it is a clothing for a…a…a 'getting better.'" He paused. "She says this style in her tradition is to...uh...how to say... to fix a balance that is inside"—and here Kaiphet put a hand on his heart. He paused again. "She…uh…says she has been weaving this piece since the end of rice harvest—about two months."

The woman continued to weave, sending her worn wooden shuttle back and forth on the silk warp threads and hand-picking the bright added colors. Another older woman appeared from a home behind the first; in her left hand she held a few folded textiles. She said something quick and sharp to the two boys, and one dashed off towards where the elder had come from. An older girl brought out a plastic pitcher of water and three glasses, and we all took a turn refreshing ourselves.

Two more people arrived—a toothless bent man wearing black-framed glasses and a young woman with an empty backpack basket who appeared at least eight months pregnant. They stood off to the side, joining the now-dozen children, and watched intently.

Maren had a flood of questions, and Kaiphet did his best:

The silk? "Raised here in the baskets woven by her father, under these tarps. Here, take a look. …"

Two dozen of the world's finest silk weavers, all from Xam Tai, gather in Phout's home to sell their textiles.

The threads? "Hand-reeled by her aunt, who lives over there…"

The colors? "All made from the forest. The dyer lives by the bus station…"

The pattern? "This one was shaped by her grandmother and has been woven many times…"

The weaver? "Her mother, this woman over here, taught her to weave when she was seven years old…"

Other women and children gathered to watch and listen, and a couple of older men, and another pitcher of water appeared. They smiled between themselves as they listened to our strange words, then to our translator's struggling enunciation, and finally the weaver's concise answer.

A stack of silk textiles appeared, and another woman unfolded a creation and held it up to her chest so we could see the full dance of her *phaa sabai*. A bevy of sharp-angled two-headed serpents dove through each other, purple over gold, in a sea of shimmering green and maroon. Maren and I laughed at the beauty and movement.

Maren asked a few more questions through Kaiphet, but the more detailed information Maren sought about the source of the silk and the meaning of the pattern proved the limit of Kaiphet's English. Kaiphet looked a bit embarrassed. "No problem," Maren said to him, "*Bo penyang.*" Kaiphet smiled at the Lao expression.

"Does she have any textiles for sale?" asked Maren, eyebrows raised. Kaiphet translated and the weaver nodded and

Kaiphet, our first guide in Xam Tai. He has remained a dear friend even though he is no longer working as a guide.

turned her head upward toward the two women on the porch. She rattled off a paragraph of information. One dashed inside, we presumed to get whatever she might have for sale. The boy who had earlier dashed into the home brought out two cheap blue plastic chairs and nodded for Maren and me to sit down.

Our boys, sensing another hour at this home, sighed, and looked around at the fifteen or so kids who surrounded them. Ari dug into his daypack and pulled out a frisbee. "Come on, Zall." The two dashed out onto the main track. The local boys watched Ari and Zall toss the frisbee three times, and then the fourth time Ari zipped the frisbee to the boy who had brought us the chairs. The boy ducked and laughed, then ran after the crashed frisbee and attempted his first-ever frisbee toss. Everyone laughed and ran to where the frisbee had landed. Maren and I knew that every boy fourteen and under would be entertained for at least half an hour.

Two more women arrived along with several more children who looked anywhere between three and twelve years old. The boys ran to join the newfound game; the girls gathered around their moms' legs and the loom. A moment later three more women came scurrying around from the road. There must now have been twenty people crowded around, not counting the dozen boys playing frisbee out in the road.

Then a bustling, weathered woman charged in shouting what sounded like instructions to all of us. Slung across her shoulders was an old worn purse so large that she almost could have fit into it herself; stuffed into the bag was a jumble of hastily folded rich-colored textiles. I think I actually *heard* Maren smile.

Our boys always carried a frisbee to share; who needs language when there's sport!

This short pugilist of a woman grabbed a silk from her purse and shook it at Maren. She shouted a few sentences—two women looked down sheepishly, and another laughed behind her hand. The original weaver returned, carefully clutching several neatly folded shimmering silks. She presented the stack to Maren with two hands and a little bow, and then stepped back, glancing at the elder.

The older woman scowled and spat out another couple of sentences. The second woman laughed again under her breath, which inspired the sour-looking elder to throw out a few more quick lines. Kaiphet chose not to translate her words; we chose not to ask.

Maren picked up one of the original weaver's silks and unfurled the opulent body-height tapestry. Rich gold threads, highlighted with sparks of deep green and blue, detailed the popular *siho* (mythical elephant-lion) motif. Ancestor figures, each riding the siho's back, shimmered in the sun. Maren took her time to admire the piece with her eyes and hands, chortling subtle "oohs" and other under-the-breath accolades at the complex artistry.

The elder, eyes blinking rapidly, waited perhaps five seconds, and she shook out one of her textiles and pushed it into Maren's hands. She spoke in a rushed high tone. No translator was needed to tell us what she wanted.

Maren politely directed the elder's textile to the side, all the while nodding and smiling. As politely as possible, Maren ignored the elder's interruption and addressed the original weaver: *"Sii tomasat? Sii chemi?"* ("Natural color? Chemical color?")

*"Sii tomasat!"* the woman grinned, surprised at Maren's Lao. The elder threw out another couple of quick lines—one of the words was tomasat—and then she burst out laughing. The other women all smiled.

*"Mai Lao? Mai Viet?"* Maren continued. (Lao silk? Vietnam silk?) The elder pushed a second textile at Maren, and Maren continued to ignore her, directing her full attention to the original weaver.

*"Mai Lao,"* the woman answered proudly. She then rattled a sentence off to Maren, who turned to Kaiphet.

"Sorry," said Kaiphet, who was watching the frisbee game. And he turned to the woman and asked her to repeat. He laughed. "She says you speak good Lao."

The elder grabbed a third textile from her purse and held it directly in Maren's vision. Maren turned toward the scowling woman and explained in English, and a flurry of hand signals, that while she would get a turn, we were currently talking with this other woman. Kaiphet didn't translate Maren's words, but he did say something short that got everyone, save the elder, to crack a smile. The elder, unperturbed, yanked now a fourth textile from her purse and held it up to Maren. Maren and she locked eyes.

The elder squinted, and pushed up her lower lip to form a deep frown. She held her grim mouth in a deep frown firmly for a moment, as if daring Maren. And then, finally with Maren's full attention, she erupted into a wide smile.

Grinning there in front of all the other women and Maren on that first day, Sukkhavit—for that is the elder's name—held that clutched textile up for Maren to see. The women all paused, waiting to see how the stand-off would end. Maren raised her eyebrows at Sukkhavit, and then she too joined the wide grin. Sukkhavit chortled as if a great secret had been shared—and maybe it had. She reached up and shook Maren by the shoulder, as if waking her up. Then they laughed together.

Sukkhavit didn't let go of Maren's shoulder.

Through Kaiphet, Maren patiently assured Sukkhavit that her silks would be also admired and, possibly, purchased. Since she had arrived after the others, she explained, it would only be appropriate that she receive our focused attention after the others. Sukkhavit scowled as she watched young Kaiphet struggle to explain and, long before he could finish, she charged off on another quick sentence. The entire group of locals tried to suppress a laugh.

Sukkhavit grimaced and coughed and threw out one-liners throughout the forty-five minutes that we examined the textiles of the others. We purchased several, and rejected several, and, because no one shared a poorly-made textile, we made sure to purchase at least one piece from each woman. With everyone's presentation came a sharp comment from Sukkhavit, most of which elicited a suppressed laugh from at least one person.

By now it was obvious that this elder was the center of village politics. She had a reputation—perhaps, indeed, a dominance—that needed to be re-stated and learned given the new social venue of having us in town. Now she was firmly in the center, in control, making untranslated comments on every piece as we unfolded it.

Finally, it was Sukkhavit's turn.

It turned out that Sukkhavit did have some of the most flawless and dynamic silks of anyone. Every piece she presented seemed rich and deep; each carried a special luster. They were, quite frankly, the finest we had seen yet in the region—or anywhere else, for that matter.

Sukkhavit.

We could tell she knew that as well.

Sukkhavit cackled with each piece of hers we set aside to purchase. She rattled off paragraphs of talk, rarely stopping for Kaiphet to stumble through a basic decoding.

A delicious feast served at Phout's home: boiled chicken, fresh mustard greens and bamboo shoots, broth from the greens, and sticky rice.

And suddenly Sukkhavit was treating Maren as if they were old friends.

Indeed, both Sukkhavit and Maren seemed to have seen that each other's take-charge exterior masked an inner soft spot. And both had much to gain with a good relationship.

In ten minutes, we had bought nearly every silk she had in her purse. (The few we rejected were presented to us by Sukkhavit again the next day, deep in a stack of new things. If nothing else, Sukkhavit is determined.)

Ten minutes after that, all four of us, along with Kaiphet, were sitting on pillows on the deliciously cool floor of Sukkhavit's home, a pitcher of filtered water and a bunch of tree-ripened bananas and tamarind pods in front of us.

Sukkhavit's home is built of well-rubbed teak wood and sits on stilts seven feet above the hard-pack dirt; steep steps lead up to the low-slung doorway. Wooden shutters from the windows are tied back to bring in daylight and a bit of breeze. An electric fan swings slowly back and forth, slowly sharing its breath. Like most Xam Tai homes, the room is devoid of furniture, save a chest where a tv and radio sit. Thin interior walls, also of wood, are covered with Beer Lao advertising posters and "beautiful young women" calendars from the last decade.

We chatted through Kaiphet for perhaps half an hour, with Sukkhavit leading the conversation. She spoke in sharp, short, direct sentences—not angry, but what to me sounded terse and impatient. Her face was animated, smiling big with one response, frowning deeply with the next. She took a keen interest in our two boys and seemed extra-pleased when they reached for their third banana (a young, silent niece restocking the bowl long before it was empty). She was also very interested in what we were looking for as a business, and we explained that we sought both traditional textiles and traditional craftwork, such as baskets and tools. She nodded and cut another quick line to Kaiphet.

This acerbic-sounding delivery turned out to be an invitation for all of us to join her and her family for dinner the next day with her family and other guests—come at 5 pm. It's the moment travelers always hope for—an invitation to participate on the inside—and we cheerfully agreed.

Poor Kaiphet. At that next day's dinner and extended evening, I have never seen anyone work so hard to keep up. The event started with Sukkhavit luring us with a few more choice textiles, and we selected what made sense for our budget. Like most Lao business people we have worked with over the years, she set a firm and reasonable price for each piece; we bargained just a little, and she gave just enough so we could all feel successful, but no one forgot who was truly in charge of the dealing. She then turned to a pile of other goods stacked in the corner.

Sukkhavit, always the businesswoman, apparently had scurried around town all day seeking possible items for us to buy for our business. Each item she obtained came with a presentation—no, a skit—where she demonstrated its usage. And with each skit the audience, that is everyone in the room, laughed appreciatively. Here was Sukkhavit as a Hmong farmer, picking greens and tossing them into her richly-patinaed backpack basket. Here was Sukkhavit as a Tai Daeng fisherman, stirring her small triangle net in the stream and placing the caught fish into the creel tied onto her waist. And now here was Sukkhavit the healing shaman, dancing a hop-step and shaking her bamboo "spirit-sticks" as if in a trance (and she actually had obtained a traditional scarf with bamboo "healing-sticks" attached from a local shaman).

Sukkhavit teaches Zall how to use a local, hand-made crossbow on our first visit to Xam Tai in 2008.

Thankfully for Kaiphet, little translation was necessary during the presentation; laughter is understood everywhere. Sukkhavit's husband, a kind man whose smile grows in proportion to the number of textiles purchased, passed me a shot glass of lao-lao, local rice whiskey, and he flicked his wrist in front of me to indicate I should toss it down in one gulp. I returned the empty glass and it was refilled and passed to the person next to me, and so on around the circle twice, and then again twice, everyone sharing the glass. Our boys, getting a nod from Maren and me, joined the toast.

Out of the corner of my eye I caught Sukkhavit luring eleven-year-old Zall over to a wooden crossbow—what kid doesn't like a handmade weapon! We had seen many boys in the area use such tools to catch rodents and small birds for dinner. Sukkhavit carefully showed Zall how to hold the crossbow, and then drew an eighteen-inch arrow from a woven bamboo sheath. She pointed to a corner of the room—perhaps to where the bamboo rat was to be—and helped Zall pull the string to a tight locked position and then load the lethal weapon. Zall aimed and Sukkhavit leaned over his shoulder like an umpire behind a catcher—her eyes, as were Zall's, trained on the target. "P-shewwww," Sukkhavit whistled as if the arrow had been launched (and here for a moment I thought she would actually let him launch the thing). She laughed and clapped Zall on the back, and then leaned over and gave him a quick grandma-like hug. Not a word had been translated; not a meaning had been missed.

"A-li," Sukkhavit said to Ari from across the room, and she shuffled over to him. With her hands she motioned for him to stand up. Ari got up slowly from his cross-legged position, and, as he maneuvered his feet under himself, Sukkhavit leaned back in mock amazement at his rising frame—at fourteen years old he was a full head taller than she was.

She flapped her hand ceremoniously several times as if preparing to perform a magic trick, and then she reached up and grabbed Ari's shoulder in a firm clutch. The room turned quiet as everyone watched.

There was a moment of profound silence. She stared up at him with a faux-serious face and with her chin jutted out and cleared her throat. She ran her eyes over him from top to bottom, bottom to top, as

Sukkhavit and Maren in 2009. Opposite inset: Zall and Ari in Xam Tai District with a Hmong elder. We have been so graciously welcomed by so many people in Houaphan Province.

if inspecting a soldier, or a side of beef.

She rattled off a quick couple sentences, and I can only catch the words for "son" (*luk sai*). The room burst into laughter, and she continued her inspection. Ari smirked, and looked a little embarrassed. A woman sitting on the floor tossed a quick line, and then more laughter, and then another said something in an undertone and everyone laughed again. Sukkhavit's firm face finally burst into a wide grin.

"She says. . ."Kaiphet smiled, and then he hesitated a moment, gathering his words. "Sukkhavit says Ari is strong and handsome . . . and would make good husband. She asks if maybe you leave him here, and he can find a Lao wife—one who can weave well."

Everyone watched us intently, smiling and eager, while Kaiphet translated for us, and then we all laughed together on the shared joke.

Suddenly everyone stood. *"Kinh, kinh"* (eat, eat) ordered Sukkhavit, and the stacks of textiles and back pillows were pushed to the edges of the room. A young woman, one of Sukkhavit's many nieces, rolled a blue fiberglass tarp about two feet wide and ten feet long onto the floor—the tablecloth. Pillows were re-distributed, Maren and I each getting two—perhaps as marks of honor, or perhaps because we bear bigger bottoms.

Out from the back-room kitchen came steaming bowlfuls of *laap* (minced pork with banana flower, garlic, ginger and chili), boiled chicken (we were honored with the chicken's head and Maren did her best with it), chicken broth with onion and garlic greens, bowls of fresh, sweet spinach-like greens, plates of steamed bamboo shoots, and several woven basketfuls of glutinous "sticky" rice. We sat cross-legged on the floor, and Sukkhavit and her family made sure that the bowls of shared food at our end of the table were refilled long before they approached empty.

Here's a cultural tip for Laos: Don't finish your portion. Because you can't. An empty guest plate is the sign of a neglected guest, and you will be served food until you leave food untouched in front of yourself. Others will even politely do without to make sure you, as a guest, have too much. And don't keep nibbling at the food once you're full. Everyone is compelled to continue eating if a guest is still eating. Finish eating, leave leftovers, and be done. So everyone else can be done, too.

On that first evening I'm sure Sukkhavit shared about her family, but we kept no notes and we were all gabbing and striving for basic understandings … and all relying on our dear poor twenty-two-year-old translator Kaiphet for anything that couldn't be mimed.

So many people were introduced—even ten years later we get faces and names mixed up, and often can't remember who is related to whom.

After dinner we shared songs back and forth from our cultures—their beautiful and haunting Lao songs of love and friendship oddly balanced with our choice of nursery rhymes (although, in truth, a round of "Row, Row, Row Your Boat" went over quite well).

Heads were drooping by 9 pm—dawn arrives early every day. With a dozen goodbyes and well wishes, we donned our headlamps and wove our way back to our simple guesthouse. Kaiphet walked with us, finally able to be silent.

"I think we've been adopted," Maren laughed quietly to everyone.

I could feel the smiles around.

## IN BETWEEN THE LINES

HERE'S THE SITUATION: I'm staring into a smiling man's eyes. He has missing teeth and crooked glasses. In his shaking hand, he offers me a glass of *lao-lao* (traditional rice whiskey). My brain freezes. Can I? Should I? Would my parents be mad? Would I insult my host? I take in the smile on his face, the cautious look on my dad's face, the hungry look on my mom's face, and the oblivious look on my brother's face. If I do decide to take the shot of rice whiskey, do I sip it? Or do I go bottoms up? What would be appropriate? My thoughts are whirling around in my head. The look on my host's face is encouraging. What do I do?

In this situation I normally make some strange noise between a yes and a no and look at my parents for advice. I'm fourteen; I'm underage, not supposed to drink until I'm twenty-one. My parents look distracted and they may have had one too many lao-lao: mom's cheeks are getting rosy and dad's stupid grin is trying to refuse another drink…they won't be too much help. If I drink, will I test my family's boundaries? If I don't, will I insult my host?

I'm in a strange place in my life. I am both a child and an adult. Both international and American. Both traveler and student. What seem like simple questions can, in reality, be confusing and controversial cultural conundrums. When do I sit down or stand? Do I eat or wait for my host?

Sukkhavit is a good friend in the village of Xam Tai, Laos, whom we go to see every time we travel. When we meet, it may be for the first time in almost a year. This year, she looked so short. Do I offer the formal way of saying hello by putting my hands together in a prayer-like "sabaidee" and offering a little bow? Or are we good enough friends to put our arms around each other? In truth, we end up in some awkward position with one of us extending a hand while the other attempts a hug. Luckily, Laos is a fairly relaxed country as far as customs go.

These questions arrive multiple times a day in the travel-world, and truthfully, the guidebooks can only tell you so much. When you're facing a cultural or social issue, your mind stops working. In the end, you wind up staring into your host's eyes with a blank look until he puts the glass in your hand and begins a toast.

*—Zall Hirschstein, age 14*

CHAPTER TWO

# Sukkhavit

XAM TAI, the regional "district capital," has a number of important leaders. There is the district governor and his family, and the district vice-governor and family. There is the head of Xam Tai's branch of the Lao Development Bank. And there are important business leaders, such as Souksakone, whom you will meet shortly. But no one seems quite as central as Sukkhavit.

Only in hindsight did we recognize that on our first day in Xam Tai—when Sukkhavit charged in and "took hold" of the situation—we had publicly, albeit unknowingly, challenged Sukkhavit by having her go last in front of the other village weavers. Neither Maren nor I had ever paused to imagine the complexity of the lifelong relationships these village residents maintained, and how that might affect our ability to connect with the artists beyond being a source of sales. But ever-sharp, Sukkhavit, in her inimitable way, managed to confirm her role, flex her will, and embrace the opportunity. And in so doing, she embraced our family.

She has been a clever and effective leader, and her scrappy efficiency, take-charge surety, and wise desire to embrace life's colors has placed her center stage in town. Which she revels in.

Granted, by 2016 her gait has slowed a bit, and she has turned over much of her business concerns to her niece, Phout. But she still nourishes an irascible charm, and can still command a laugh acting as the ham. She can still throw daggers with a glance.

On every visit Sukkhavit makes sure she sees us on the day of our arrival, often arriving on the back of a young relative's motorcycle. She'll bustle up to Maren and wrap an arm around her, leaning in, her head tucking under Maren's armpit. She'll chuckle about how tall and wide Maren is, and then ask about the two boys and "grandma" (my mom, who visited with us in 2010).

Sukkhavit speaks with a strong Xam Tai accent; she would say "Xam-Tuh," her "ai" spit out as a short "uh," as in "book" which makes her rapid-fire talk a challenge to translators unfamiliar with the district. But with Sukkhavit, at least for us, her words appear simultaneously spoken and acted. We enjoy each other's company, even when the words aren't translated. Of course, after ten years of sharing meals, sales, looks, lao-lao, songs, ceremony, and stories of our families and lives, the pleasant warmth of seeing a dear friend needs no translation.

Sukkhavit was born in 1952 in Xam Tai to a family that tended productive, flat farmland, and she remembers as a child having to work in the rice fields during Spring's planting season and Fall's harvest, just as many families still do today. Like many young girls, she began weaving at age six or seven, and she spent her first years spinning and weaving cotton *sinh*, which were worn by all the local women at the time. She admits her mother was not a good weaver, but others in the village recognized Sukkhavit's talent and nurtured her skills. By age eight she was entrusted to weave with silk, and she wove many *tiin sinh*—the decorative embroidered silk strip sewn onto a sinh's bottom hem.

As she approached adolescence, war overtook the region. She recalls having to live in lean-to shelters in the jungle, as a thatched-roof home by the fields was nothing but a target for the bombers. She recalls building makeshift shelters, and having to dig a tunnel near her temporary jungle home for the family to hide in when the bombs fell; she recalls farming the rice and vegetable fields under the cover of nightfall. She did continue to weave during wartime,

Sukkhavit dons one of her own silk shoulder cloths which she wove.

At age 66, Sukkhavit still spends ample time at her loom. Opposite: A masterful piece woven by Sukkhavit.

using tree trunks to hold the warp tension on a makeshift loom. She remembers that in 1968 at age sixteen, she began to sell her textiles locally.

Her marriage was delayed until the war's end in 1975—she laughs that she was now "too old to get married," but fortunately she found affection and comfort in her partner of forty-one years, a hard-working gentleman who also grew up in Xam Tai. They have eight children, all grown, only one of whom is still dependent: her youngest son who studies at the university in Vientiane. Two of her daughters live in Xam Tai, and all of her daughters, she says with pride, know how to weave.

After the war, she settled down to lead a weaver's life—she laughs now that her energy and drive when she was younger were "like a fever." Often cotton and silk were not available in the market, and often there was no money whatsoever, and thus she chose to raise and process both the cotton and silk needed for creating textiles; she learned from other locals how to make the natural dyes. As her children grew to be old enough to weave cotton and silk, she turned more attention to raising, reeling, and dyeing silk to make sure her family had enough silk thread to continue being successful weavers.

In 1988, a westerner—one of the rare white faces to be seen in Xam Tai since the French occupied the region in the mid-1950s—approached Sukkhavit about making textiles for import. He provided a design for a sinh in a pattern she had never seen before. In fact, it was an old-style sinh of the Tai Dam people (Sukkhavit is Lao Loum), but Sukkhavit jumped on a market opportunity. The gentleman returned to buy the textiles she and her family wove in this design for the next two years, but then he was never seen again.

Sukkhavit mentions that this has happened now several times—an outsider arrives all excited, gets a little business rolling, and then disappears. She laughs at the memory, and then tells us straight out that Maren and I have been the one exception—that is, we've kept coming back, now going on ten years. And that is why she has so

Water buffalo graze on the banks of the Nam Xam. Opposite: A man/woman healing cloth woven by Sukkhavit.

much trust in our effort. She reminds us that friendship is an emotional commitment, and not something that turns on, and then off.

Ironically, that Tai Dam sinh pattern ended up being a boon to Sukkhavit and her Lao Loum family. Beginning in the early 1990s the market for selling textiles began to open up in the urban centers of Luang Prabang and Vientiane, and Sukkhavit found good success selling these Tai Dam–style sinh in these marketplaces. Sukkhavit also started re-creating some of the traditional Lao Loum and Tai Daeng textiles, foreseeing the developing market in handwoven silks.

Travel restrictions were further lifted in the mid-1990s, and soon a trickle of Australian, Japanese, and French textile tourists started visiting Xam Tai, and Sukkhavit took center stage as a regional expert in weaving and dyeing textiles and getting them to market. A generous donation from one Australian enthusiast allowed Sukkhavit to invest in new materials, including new looms for both her family and the growing network of weavers eager to access a developing market.

Her "fever-like" energy propelled her to the front of the craft, art, and business that was re-emerging after a half-century of war and isolation. By 2007, when she first invited us into her home, she was a leading elder promoting Xam Tai region's highest quality hand-reeled, naturally-dyed silks.

Today she is no longer in the middle of the business, having trained and handed off the reins of leadership, marketing, and momentum to her very capable niece, Phout (who lives two houses over, and whom you will meet soon). Sukkhavit now spends more time with her grandchildren, and she still likes to sit in the shade of her home at her loom, eyes peering over her glasses, sliding her worn shuttle across the warp and picking the colors for a new temple-cloth.

She expresses a profound hope that textile creation will continue to improve the lives of everyone in her family, and she bursts with pride when she speaks of the youngest weavers—those who are six or seven—who participate in the textile tradition and economy of her village.

CHAPTER THREE

# The *Falang*, and How We Got Here

MAREN AND I did not anticipate a life of silks, or Lao friends. That was a surprise foisted on us in our middle years.

We met when we were fifteen and sixteen, as 'cello stand partners in high school orchestra. Maren had grown up with a home-economics teacher for a mother. Her basement was full of looms, dye materials and sewing projects, all performed and taught with Germanic precision.

Our social lives overlapped and, several years later, at the end of college, we found our affection with each other. We worked and flirted in Seattle, and then I took advantage of an opportunity to teach English in Kathmandu, Nepal. Distance, in our case, did make the heart grow fonder, and Maren joined me for the second half of the year-long teaching adventure.

Unpredictable adventure surely bonds people. In our case of backpack travel, however, the romance of cuddling together at 16,000 feet in the warm sunshine under inspirational Nepali peaks, tempered the next night with washing a partner's vomit from a towel in a sub-freezing stream by dim headlamp, also created stories that can't be forgotten, and knots that can't be unwound without unraveling some essential fabric. Did we even know we were weaving our lives together?

We moved back to Seattle. Maren worked the 8 to 5 with a nonprofit that assisted companies disrupted by international trade inequities. I substitute-taught and tutored, and then I spent a year at Berkeley obtaining a master's degree in writing education, intent on teaching at the high school level. A year later—a marriage, and then another year of bonding that included the better part of a year exploring much of what was in between west China's deserts and Indonesia's swamps and islands.

We chose to settle in Eugene, Oregon, eager to find a balance between our rural fantasies and our urban realities. I founded a private tutoring service, which I still direct twenty-seven years later; Maren brought her project-management skills to a marketing company, and then the medical insurance world. We bought an old farmhouse with a couple of acres to raise chickens, vegetables, and, it turns out, our sons: Ari, who arrived in 1993, and Zall, who joined three years later. Comfortable, predictable.

Then life threw a curve ball—or perhaps a better metaphor would be a "snarled warp." Maren had to leave a much-loved career path to find "better balance"—a euphemism understood by anyone who struggles with a depressive disorder. For a time darkness hid the colors, and gray was

Opposite: Xam Tai's beautiful valley. The town of Xam Tai can be seen on the far side of the valley nestled under the hills. Below: The main road into Xam Tai.

Josh and the boys in 2009, with bags of purchased textiles, wait for the next vehicle with ample room to get us "down the road."

a texture.

In 2005, with Maren's dark veil lifting and our confidences re-emerging, we decided to take a six-week backpack-style trip with our sons, now ages twelve and nine—because we could. Here was the long-dreamed-of time for the next "Asia adventure"; opportunity sometimes is, and then isn't—best taken advantage of while it's possible.

Plus, we'd been told that kids "grow up fast so take advantage when you can." There they are, and then, so suddenly, they're not kids anymore. A dozen years later, we'll confirm that is the truth.

We chose to visit Southeast Asia for its ease and familiarity, Bangkok being a familiar entry point. With a family agreement that we take no electronics (only books and our own imaginations served for escape), we spent some delicious time on Thailand's Koh Chang with snorkels in hand, and then wandered, unattached to any tourist agency, through Cambodia and up the coast of Vietnam, essentially making up each day's itinerary but not wanting to push too vigorously. We sought both popular attractions like Angkor Wat and untouristed places like our private visit to a stilt village on Tonle Sap. We enjoyed "home stay" experiences on the Mekong Delta and again in northern Vietnam's Lao Cai Province. We ate local street-food for most meals—fresh, unique, delicious, and often a story in itself.

We found, as a family, that the more unusual the event, the odder the food, and the stranger the experience—well, the more fun we had. Indeed, Maren and I, with our two boys, climbed right into a wonderful and invigorating "traveler's zone." We reminded ourselves from our previous travels (and taught our kids) that all adventures are fated to end well—if for nothing other than the story you get to own. Getting lost, eating the weird whatever and "going with the day" each becomes a goal in itself. You just never know what might be around the next corner.

The kids were great travelers—willing to try every strange food, whether fruit or insect. There's the "leech" story, the "falling-through-the-chief's-deck" story, the "eighteen-hour-bus-ride-with-three-breakdowns" story, the "bad stomach cramps" story, and other tales we'll forever embellish. There's also learning to trust that no matter what, it always works out. As it always did, and does.

Also, our experiences reinforced that people are, in the grand whole, kind, helpful, empathetic, and generous. This proved itself day in and day out when kind strangers stepped up to make our day richer. It still proves itself true.

To add shape to our venture, Maren packed her love of color and handcrafted art, and that led us to seek places and people who were making things—not "knickknack" stuff for tourists, but "real" stuff, like the straw brooms the grandmothers used to raise the dust in front of their homes, or the bamboo water-buffalo bells that rattle in the paddy fields. Maren especially lusted after handwoven textiles and the older tools and baskets that wear the rich patina of genuine use. Still today, when we explore new territory, we always first ask where to find local people who make things. This assuredly creates a path for an adventure.

On that first trip in 2005, our flight from Hanoi to Vientiane flew over northern Laos, and I vividly remember looking out the airplane window and seeing nothing but rugged ridges of unscathed land—dense green waves of ridge after ridge with rare splashes of brown designating a tiny village. It seemed so raw and unexplored compared to the endlessly terraced and diesel-fueled productivity of crowded Vietnam.

Upon our return home, we recognized that once again, "backpack-style travel" was creating tight and intricate bonds, this time for our family of four. We vowed to return for another venture and carved out a similar

Cows graze on the rice terraces in the dry, winter season.

The rugged hills of Houaphan Province are steep, steamy, and smoky with the slash and burn preparations for the monsoon planting season to come.

vacation schedule the following year, 2006. This time we spent nearly five weeks in northern Laos, traveling by local bus, river canoe, private taxi, motorcycle, and on foot. We spent many nights as the sole guests (along with a hired local guide) in remote rural villages. The scenery was, and is, incredible, with steep twisty jungle terrain; it is rugged, and isolating. From a westerner's standpoint, it all felt so unexplored and undeveloped. Even today, we will spend a week in easily-accessed Xam Tai and see no other falang or hear any English spoken outside our own words.

After our family's second Asia adventure, we felt emboldened and healthy—perhaps a little cocky. "Start a little business," some friends said. "You bring back such amazing stuff." Jeez—it sounded like an exciting adventure in itself!

So we did. "Perhaps it can pay for another trip?" we imagined. And it nearly did.

So Maren quit her part-time "recovery job" and we turned to learning everything we could about customs brokers, importing, and labeling laws. We explored abebooks.com and devoured every text we could find on the cultures and the textiles of the Annamite Mountain region of northern Laos and Vietnam. "You do it or you don't," we told ourselves.

And we made some decisions, taking into account the realities of parenting and managing a stable home, about how we best liked to spend our personal, valuable time and effort. (Money, I preach to my kids, comes and goes. Time, however, only goes. Spend it wisely.)

We continued also to explore the cotton, hemp, batik, and other textile arts found in Laos's northern and southern provinces as well as across the border in northern Vietnam where we have also developed some wonderful and enduring relationships with several Hmong and Dzao weavers and embroiderers.

Maren, in a moment of inspiration (and under the pressure of succumbing to a numbing "International Woven Arts, Inc.") titled us "Above the Fray: Traditional Hilltribe Art." "We are," we cheered, "Above the Fray at last!" (We acknowledge the choice of the common term "Hilltribe" crudely lumps together an incredibly diverse and rich array of traditions, languages, histories, perspectives, and needs. Our apologies if this term for you connotes any sense of cultural stereotyping or belittling.)

Indeed, we had found what we anticipated to be an engaging, dynamic business, which could work (sort of) with the schedule of running a tutoring service and having two kids in school, and that also energized and gave context to Maren's passion with color and creative design.

Maren and Josh examine and choose textiles in Phout's home with a group of local weavers. Malaithong, our translator and guide, is next to Josh.

We had found an excuse for backpack-style rural ventures in Asia with the kids for years to come. (And both our boys traveled with us until each went to college.)

We also had gained an excuse to deepen our cultural experiences. This element of connecting with the locals was no longer a fantasy, but a business requirement—and expense. We *needed* to make relationships with the artists of the region. (*Oh, the riches we found here!*)

We even had an excuse to shop—for the business, of course. Eyes always peeled, every day on the road. Every village has treasures and stories. We quickly learned that "traveling with purpose" is immensely more fun than just wandering.

"And it would be good for college admissions," we justified. (It turned out, by the way, we were right.)

Perhaps most of all: it would feel healthy and momentous to weave a new pattern—to create lives that lifted rather than entrenched. That created, rather than endured. That dove in, rather than scanned. That engaged and flowed, rather than sat and puddled.

Maren is *alive* when she is "on the venture." All her natural enthusiasm and curiosity comes to the surface in a broad smile and almost-too-loud guffaw; her earnestness to bridge is magnetic. Her rich colors dance like one of Sukkhavit's vibrant silk tapestries. To see her fully alive again was—is—the greatest gift.

And, of course, we really had very little idea what we were doing or getting into, which made the whole idea seem possible.

CHAPTER FOUR

# Spark

IF ONE IS going to promote and sell fine silks, one had better know silk textiles. For our business, that seemed like a reasonable expectation, and a decent starting point.

So what are the criteria for a well-woven textile?

Everything handwoven is something unique unto itself, for it took a particular person his or her own time and effort to create. How then were we to determine what items and whose time and effort is of "greater merit"?

Should we measure it by its creative qualities, or by virtues related to its acquisition or its provenance? Can one artist's reputation trump another's inspiration? Do we measure what it takes? What it means? How it feels? How it "sings"? How it ages? Its cost?

Should we quantify complexity? Or flawlessness? Or degree of tradition or modernity?

And who are we, here in the role of enthusiasts and business owners, to draw the boundaries of an art and grant valuation?

Well, given that we were taking on the tasks of what had to be a self-sustaining business, we felt obligated to establish a set of criteria to better measure and compare.

A well-woven, collectible and desirable silk textile has:

**Texture and drape:** A quality silk textile has weight and integrity, and the gifts that Nature offers in this fiber are reflected in both the shimmer and weight. In Xam Tai, this is emblematic of the roles of the sericulturist and reeler, who raise and prepare Nature's threads for its next quality:

**Richness and vibrancy**: A well-woven textile expresses itself in hues and tones that shape our perception. The emblematic role for these qualities is that of the natural-dye artist, who blends tradition and chemistry with patience and insight and prepares the threads for their role in expressing the next quality:

**Meaning over time:** A quality textile allows tradition to hold sway, but does not hesitate to bring the wisdom of the art in contact with the spirit of today. This quality is symbolized by the designer and template-maker, who shapes the outlines of each design, aligning purpose with form, in preparation for the next quality:

**Precision and consistency:** Quality textiles are accurate, tight, and sharp. Every

A rich combination of color, pattern, sheen, texture, and drape set the silks of Xam Tai apart.

thread is well placed; every point of tension and transition of color is sure and intended. This is the role of the weaver herself, pulling the threads of all the other qualities into a textile's primary expression:

**Authenticity and pragmatism:** The finished textile will fulfill its role as is evidenced by its power, economy, and purpose. Authenticity allows uniqueness to survive in a cool business world that exerts great effort to pull to a common, predictable center. Pragmatism assures the effort bears fruit, and that the task and tradition both remain relevant. This role is fulfilled by the market, and the ultimate bearer and user of the textile.

And then finally, there is:

**Spark:** An ephemeral quality that speaks not to numbers but to passions—a quality that looks at the whole and finds a unique articulation and vibrancy. In a textile with Spark, one can see a step beyond the other measured qualities to an exclusive charisma, a heartfelt embrace of color and texture and pattern, an extra "pop" and pizzazz. Spark treasures the difference between excellence and love.

And we swear, with a little practice, you can sense the Spark in a quality textile.

A single passing reference in Lonely Planet's Laos travel guide offers that the village of Xam Tai, in northeastern Laos's Houaphan Province, is a place renowned for handwoven textiles. As the village was only a few hours' bus ride from Xam Neua, where we were in 2007, and as the route promised to weave between scenic terraced hills and an untamed corner of the Nam Xam Wilderness Area, and as we indeed had two to three days for an adventure, we hired a local translator from the tourist office, Kaiphet, and off our family of four went to meet Sukkhavit.

That was the first trip with our business in mind—and we had carried a bag of kip notes (each 50,000-kip note then worth about $5) in our luggage to back up the plan. It seemed simple enough: we'd go to the villages that focus on weaving and other traditional arts, buy the stuff at a reasonable local rate, ship it home, and sell it for enough to "turn the wheel" so the process could be repeated. Hope held that it might turn a modest profit, but we also understood that we were guaranteed to gain a unique experience.

Lun (see chapter 12) holds up one of her *phaa phi mon* masterpieces.

We had initially, and naively, anticipated that we would connect with dozens of villages over time—continuing in Laos and Vietnam, but also extending out to exploring further reaches beyond Laos and Vietnam—perhaps Myanmar and on to eastern India's remote Nagaland district. The information age only fuels such fantasies.

In 2007, perhaps a dozen of Houaphan's towns, including Muang Vaen, Nam Noen, Saleui, and Ban Nakham, wove textiles primarily using locally-raised, hand-reeled, naturally-dyed silk and handspun cotton. Each of these towns also created a variety of textile types, from the practical sinh to useful door curtains to the elaborate ceremonial pieces. Each community seemed to be searching for a market by creating the breadth of their traditional textiles.

What we did not know in 2007 is how rare the textiles were that we first encountered. Somehow, they just seemed right there when we reached out. Weren't there dozens of villages and districts creating such finery?

In fact: No, there weren't. And aren't.

Today, in 2016, we notice that all four of the above-named villages are increasingly using factory-spun silk or synthetic fibers purchased in the market to form the warp and weft, and the art of natural dyeing is quickly succumbing to the ease of market-purchased chemical dyes.

But we perceived none of this in 2007, and in that first buying trip, we had already visited a half-dozen villages in Houaphan Province that produced an array of exquisite traditional cloths. Surely there were more yet to be discovered . . . Surely . . . .

Oddly enough, we had stumbled onto the "mother lode" in that first season, at our first claim. For indeed, Sukkhavit's Xam Tai is *the* unique and vital center for traditional, naturally-dyed woven silk.

We now laugh that "the gods" played a wonderful and cruel joke on us—dangling the best first to get us to swallow the hook, line, and sinker on first gulp. Whatever the source of our fortune, the gods continue, ten years later, to entice us forward.

The surest lure consisted of a series of fortunate contacts that started, unbeknownst to us, the moment we bought a silk from Sukkhavit. Indeed, starting with Sukkhavit, we have had the unanticipated pleasure of befriending some of the most generous, loyal, and creative people we have ever had the pleasure to meet. And these people, it turns out, just "happen" to be in the center of the most recognized and talented independent silk artists in Laos, and perhaps the world.

*"Maren is half Lao," the women of Xam Tai now laugh. "She is our sister," they proclaim. "Move here and learn how to weave," they beckon with smiles.*

The following year, in 2008, our translator, Kaiphet, was attending a tourism training in China and unavailable. Thankfully, the Government Tourism Office in Xam Neua was able to recommend another office worker, Malaithong, who had excellent English and who, lo and behold, just happened to have grown up in Xam Tai and still had family there. Yes, agreed Malaithong, she would be happy to be hired as our translator and "cultural liaison" for the extended weekend, provided she could bring her four-year-old son, Bingo. We eagerly agreed, excited to get an "inside" guide—someone who could introduce us to people she knew in the community.

The sheer volume of silk textiles produced by the weavers of Xam Tai speaks to a long history of skill-building and industry.

# two. Setting

*The tropical setting; the sound of the language;*
*the scent of the bamboo fire; the mannerisms of our hosts;*
*the shared smiles and stares.*
*Meeting someone new carries all the*
*anticipation of an unknown blossom.*

*What colors will emerge? What shape will take form?*
*How long is the season?*

*Do its roots get nourished? Or do they wither and return to*
*the nameless earth that we tread and trust each day.*

tion zones" into pudding. Going west from Xam Neua follows a rugged route to Vietnam; the venture to Hanoi takes anywhere from sixteen to thirty hours, depending on a long list of "whatevers." A now-being-rebuilt road promises improvement, just as it has for several years.

Summer is the warm monsoon season, with temperatures eager to climb above 90°F (32°C) with high humidity—sometimes really high humidity. Afternoons can be scorching and dripping at the same time. Winters usually offer delicious "tee shirt" afternoons, but evening temperatures can dip to 40°F (4°C). In 2016, it even snowed! Bring a heavy jacket—the winter's cold is inescapable as there is no central heating, not even in Xam Neua's fanciest accommodations.

The modest *Nam Xam*, or Xam River, flows clear through Xam Neua, right past the new market, then meanders through narrow valleys and terraced rice fields, eventually rushing through the protected Nam Xam Wilderness Area southward to re-emerge in the beautiful bowl-shaped Xam Tai Valley. It then tumbles southeast, through Ban Tao, and another sixty miles (100 km) through Vietnam to the South China Sea. Small hydroelectric projects, some under construction, some planned on paper, and some still in the dream phase, are spurring development. Laos, one of the most cash-poor nations on Earth, anticipates and is preparing for the emerging power demand from neighboring China and Vietnam.

To get to Houaphan's southern Xam Tai and Meung Kuan Districts and the heart of Laos's silk-weaving tradition requires a seven-hour bus ride from Xam Neua—four hours if you hire an impatient private driver with a high-clearance vehicle. The narrow sealed road goes east through the rapidly developing town of Vieng Xai (where the Pathet Lao founded modern Laos's government, hence the development) and then, a few kilometers before reaching the Vietnam border town of Na Meo, a side road climbs southward and weaves through the high ridges of the Nam Xam Wilderness Area to finally reach Xam Tai.

Technically, Phonsavan is Xam Tai's district center (not to be confused with Phonsavan, capital of neighboring Xieng Khouang Province), but everyone refers to Phonsavan and older neighbor Xam Tai as "Xam Tai." Here one finds the secondary schools for the district, a four-year-old western-medical clinic, several guesthouses and restaurants (no menus yet), several engine repair shops, and, opening in 2015, a Lao Development Bank with an ATM. The picturesque, ramshackle low-ceilinged central market was replaced in 2014 with a new cement marketplace

A half mile farther is the village of Xam Tai, the original district center and home to about seventy-five households.

The traditional village of Xam Tai is comprised of older-style homes, each 500 to 800 square feet and set on six- or seven-foot (2 m) posts. Most of the homes have painted wood siding and corrugated roofs rather than the bamboo walls and thatch roofs of many places, revealing the relative wealth of the local inhabitants. Inside, homes are divided into two or three separate living and sleeping areas using woven bamboo mats or wooden boards for walls. Vinyl flooring laid on top of raw wood floors is common. These homes still set their kitchen area at one end of the house in a separate area that has better ventilation, as meals are cooked over wood and bamboo flames. Above the fire on a woven mat and suspended on hooks sit various baskets and utensils, as the smoke prevents insect damage. Xam Tai is a serene village set on the banks of the beautiful Nam Xam, and the shade of its residents' homes is inviting.

The population of greater Xam Tai is perhaps 1000 people, plus perhaps another 300 kids who attend Xam Tai's secondary schools and whose parents live in outlying villages (these kids usually live with a relative, as most everyone in the district has some relative living there). Most of its population is either ethnic Tai Daeng, who are traditionally animist, or Lao Loum, who are traditionally Buddhist.

In 2012 the Xam Tai District, which is comprised of greater Xam Tai and many dozen nearby villages, was split into two halves, with the western portion now called Meung Kuan District. A new road, some eighteen miles (30 km) long, is being cut between Xam Tai and the district center—the town of Meung Kuan—that will make it accessible to car traffic. Currently, only four-wheel-drive vehicles and motorcycles can get through, and even then the road requires dry weather conditions. There is a sealed road to Meung Kuan from the Vietnam side, but that border crossing is only open to Vietnamese and Lao citizens.

Meung Kuan town is experiencing a modern makeover as it is being transformed from a sleepy, thatched-roof village to the central headquarters of a new district. Secondary schools, government office buildings, hotels, and a hospital are being built. In 2015, Maren and I slept in the only hotel—the first falang guests! The building was wired, as was much of the new town, but the town's electricity had not yet been

turned on. In 2016, electricity was available all day every day and the town was bursting with construction—perhaps another twenty modern homes were built along the newly-platted streets, and a city-wide drainage system had been completed. Several nearby villages of Lao Loum, Hmong, and other ethnic groups have relocated to this new site as well. It is the modern century, indeed.

Other, smaller villages of thirty to one hundred or more homes are sprinkled throughout the province's endless valleys and steep hills; some have dirt road access and others have motorcycle-capable trails. Most villages are affiliated with a single ethnic group (e.g. Hmong, Tai Daeng, Tai Dam, etc.), although mixed-ethnic families and communities are not uncommon. Silk and cotton weavers can be found in almost every village, although some villages, especially those of Lao Loum and Tai Daeng people (such as Xam Tai and Ban Tao), have a distinguished tradition of leading the local textile industry.

A peculiar pride does emanate from the breadth of Xam Tai's population, a trait born from a thousand years of semi-isolation and perseverance. It is as if they know they live in one of the world's most beautiful regions, and know they have the skills, talent, and tenacity to endure life's challenges—even those as horrific as war and famine—to emerge on the other side of adversity as upright as they are sure of their ancestors.

Tough times, if the people can survive at all, create a resilient community.

The main boulevard into Xam Neua, Houaphan's provincial capital.

CHAPTER SIX

# Nang Tiip of Xam Tai

The traditional, older village of Xam Tai, where we met Sukkhavit in 2007, has one broad and dusty road that is fronted by two dozen well-appointed stilt-raised homes; traffic, although light, can zip through quickly and the children tend to avoid playing on the well-groomed thoroughfare.

However, walking between two of the homes on the right—and walking close to neighbors and their homes is not considered obtrusive in small villages—we find a pot-holed alley that parallels the main road, and here one witnesses the active daily life of Xam Tai's residents: kids from toddler age to near adolescent play with sticks and bicycles, old men prepare bamboo for weaving fishing creels, young men repair their fishing nets, chickens and roosters strut for primacy, laundry waves in the light breeze.

Nearly every home has at least one floor loom set in the shade; several of the homes shade three or four looms. In the late afternoon, walking by these twenty-five or so homes, we find twenty women actively weaving. One home has three young girls weaving side by side with Lao pop music blaring from a dusty boom box.

At the end of the lively side road stands a modest home with a porch overlooking a small stream. In the cool under the home, away from the glare of the sun, sits Nang Tiip on her worn bench. She is one of the town's master weavers, a forty-one-year-old veteran dyer, spinner, and weaver.

Left: Nang Tiip wearing one of her handwoven silk shoulder cloths with a box of naga pattern. Opposite: Nang Tiip's first textile created completely on her own; she raised the silkworms, reeled the silk, created the natural dyes, designed the pattern, and wove this stunning piece.

Left: Making and repairing fish nets are ongoing tasks for the men of Xam Tai. Right: A pastoral scene along the Nam Xam.

Nang Tiip learned how to weave from her mother. At ten years of age, she was weaving cotton sinh for local women, and by age fourteen she was spinning her own cotton. As a child she also learned the intricacy of weaving silk using the discontinuous supplemental weft method, and she began her career weaving silk patterns on narrow, cotton-backed tiin sinh (skirt borders). She laughs with a big open smile as she remembers that those first tiin sihn sold pretty well in the developing marketplace.

She is married and has three children: a daughter who is twenty-three, and two sons, ages nineteen and eighteen. Yes, she laughs, of course her daughter has been taught how to dye and weave!

Nang Tiip still works with both cotton and silk. Part of the year she weaves cotton fabric, which she dyes with indigo to make men's shirts and pants. Most men wear factory-made western-style clothing, but there is still a small market for those who prefer the feel, look, and tradition of handcrafted clothing.

Most of the year, however, is spent weaving the complex ceremonial textiles, *phaa biang*. Indeed, these are the pieces that catch a fairer price in the marketplace. She has the patience and skill to be nearly flawless with her weaving, and her talent with color play, especially with jewel tones, allows her completed pieces to stand out with maturity and a certain "pop."

Nang Tiip is one of Xam Tai's most productive weavers, putting in seven to eight hours every day, and she has been a consistent talent represented in the silks our business has purchased over the years. As a matter of fact—we first met Nang Tiip at that first gathering in Sukkhavit's home.

Nang Tiip chuckles as she pushes her richly-worn wooden shuttle across the warp threads. "Yes," she answers. "I very much look forward to teaching my grandchildren how to weave someday. It is still a good way to earn a living."

The rural villages of Houaphan Province, such as Xam Tai, have a timeless, peaceful quality.

CHAPTER SEVEN

# Political History of the Region

The frustrated French colonial powers expressed a sentiment that still echoes today:

*The industrious Vietnamese plant the rice, and the Cambodians watch it grow. But the Lao? What to make of them! Indeed—they listen to the rice grow.*

*In northern Laos most especially, there is an ease, a contentment, a calm. Life afforded . . . .*

*The shade of the home beckons. The weaver looks up, nods a welcome, smiles, and returns to her craft.*

*Come and sit down, begs the afternoon. Here is an old wooden bench. Listen closely to the breeze and the cicadas.*

*Come sit in the shade and listen to the clicks and taps of the weaver at the loom. Listen to your breath—in, then a long out. Here is where you are.*

*Listen to the rich rows of deep green in the sun-massaged fields . . . Just sit, and listen . . . .*

The first people to have left a mark in the region did not leave much of a calling card. Houaphan Province's virtually unstudied Hintang Archaeological Site boasts some haunting, though underwhelming, stone menhirs thought to be the funerary remnants of a people who lived more than 2000 years ago. A province away are the ancient and unsolved giant stone vessels that dot the Plain of Jars, said to be carved 2500 years ago also by "an unknown people."

Newly-planted rice fields fill the valley floor.

That Foun, a thirty-meter-tall sixteenth-centry Buddhist stupa near the Plain of Jars. It somehow survived the bombing during the Vietnam war.

From the ninth through the fourteenth centuries, waves of ethnic migrations escaping persecution in southern China and northern Vietnam—people whom we today classify broadly as being of Lao-Tai ethnicity—sent people into the rugged Annamite Mountain valleys of what is now northern Laos. The first waves settled in the fertile region along the Mekong River of what is now Luang Prabang Province in north central Laos (forcing out the indigenous dwellers). Over the next centuries they expanded their influence southward, eventually spilling into Thailand's northern Isan region. In 1356, Fa Ngum, a Lao-Tai leader, consolidated the Kingdom of Lan Xang in what is now northern Laos, and today King Fa Ngum is celebrated as the founder of traditional Laos and the one who brought Buddhism to the region. About three million people (60 percent of Laos's total population) identify as Lao-Tai; another twenty-four million Lao-Tai people live in Thailand. The Lao Loum, as they're known now, are matrilineal adherents of Theravada Buddhism, and have been silk weavers for millennia.

The Tai Daeng (Red Tai) ethnic group, whose mythology and traditions are equally evident in Xam Tai's textiles, followed a more easterly route in their migrations in the thirteenth and fourteenth centuries, eventually settling in the mountains of what is now northwest Vietnam and northeast Laos. Today, about 25,000 people who identify as Tai Daeng live in Laos, almost all in Houaphan, and another 125,000 live across the border in Vietnam. The Tai Daeng traditionally are animists and ancestor worshipers, and they maintain, to some degree even today, a rich tradition of shamanic ritual that seeks to gain favor with or placate the spirits that inhabit our world and can affect one's well-being. Tai Daeng animism, unlike many other animist cultures, does not hold that inanimate objects have spirits in themselves, but rather that one's ancestors, acting as spirits, can inhabit and affect our natural world. The Tai Daeng, too, have an ancient tradition of being raisers, weavers, and traders of silk.

In the early fourteenth century, northeast Laos, including Houaphan and its eastern provincial neighbor, Xieng Khouang, developed as its own state, called Muang Phuan. Regional historians note that "state" is a poor word choice in that it does not reflect the unique, non-western relationships that these regional political units maintained. A Muang was an independent district, steeped to varying degrees in Buddhist, Taoist, and animist traditions, that sought not to compete for space and resources with the neighboring muang; rather, the muang strived, in its trade and politics, to co-exist in relative harmony so that, with their neighbors, they could cooperatively and adequately respond to larger outside threats and challenges.

Muang Phuan did pay tribute to Fa Ngum's Lan Xang Kingdom, as well as to regional kingdoms to the north and west (Sino-Vietnamese) and south (Siamese-Ayutthaya), each of whose influence (and borders) grew, then shrank, and then grew again as generations went by. Over the next centuries, Muang Phuan both was claimed by, and, when politically tenable, traded with the Vietnamese and the Siamese. The delicate back-and-forth of tiny Houaphan, on the geographic fence between two powerhouse cultures, perhaps is one reason that the local people seem so tolerant of others.

At the beginning of the nineteenth century, the Siamese authorities set out to de-populate Houaphan to create a "no man's land" between their expanding state and the aggressive Vietnamese. This depopulation effort relocated many Lao-Tai people to Vientiane, Bangkok, and other areas west of the Mekong River. Many in Houaphan fled the Siamese persecution and joined communities to the east, in Vietnam.

The Vietnamese controlled the heart of Houaphan for much of the nineteenth century, although the regional authorities also paid tribute to Laos's Lan Xang Kingdom to the east to avoid conflict. From 1874-1886, Chinese bandits known as Ho (or Haw) plundered and destroyed the regional cities of Xam Neua and Muang Phuan, and the ensuing chaos ultimately resulted, in 1896, with the new French colonizing authority placing Houaphan under the protection and authority of Tonkin, an Indo-Chinese state more aligned with Vietnam then Siam.

Buddhas adorn the remains of the sixteenth-century Wat Phia Wat in old Muang Phuan near the Plain of Jars.

In an effort to maintain peace, the French colonial government also instituted a policy that relocated the Buddhist-influenced ethnicities (primarily Lao Loum) to the northern and western districts of Houaphan, and the animist-influenced ethnicities (primarily Tai Daeng and Tai Dam) to the southern and eastern districts,

Remnants of the Vietnam war are visible everywhere. From left: Bomb crater sign at Plain of Jars. Boy carrying defused bombs; his family repurposes the aluminum parts. Mold for the recycled aluminum spoons sold and used throughout Laos.

including Xam Tai and Meung Kuan. Many of the current Tai Daeng families living in these southern districts originally settled about 120 years ago during this relocation. They blended with the Buddhist Lao Loum people who did not relocate.

The French were not widely seen as an aggressive, dominating power in this region; they were perceived more as a protecting power shielding, the minority peoples from the aggressive Ho and the expansive Siamese. Better the mild and distant French than the plunderers to the north and south.

However, there was one tension the French brought to northeastern Laos that is relevant to textile design. Along with French politics came Catholic missionaries. The Buddhist population of the region was adamantly opposed to conversion, whereas many in the animist population found its message persuasive. Consequently, many converted animists were placed in administrative positions of authority by the French, altering the traditional political balance. Although the ethnic groups aligned with Buddhism tried to fight this injustice, many ended up moving away, leaving Houaphan more particularly populated with Tai Daeng people. Cheesman notes that ever since this emigration of Buddhists from Houaphan Province through the 1920s, the animist motifs and styles in the regional textiles have had a more dominant influence in design than those of Buddhist tradition, a trait that persists today.

French colonization had little economic influence in Houaphan. Access was challenging, the land was neither richly productive nor resourceful, and the region had been significantly depopulated. The few tribal people who remained, including the inhabitants of the particularly isolated Xam Tai region, continued to live a life little affected or influenced by global forces.

The Japanese made a brief entry in early 1945 and insisted during their two-month stay that the king of Laos declare independence from France; many in authority were tempted, but Laos, fearful of western repercussions and under the authority of French-supported King Sisavangvong, returned to being a French protectorate. However, the seeds of an independence movement had been nourished and, in the early 1950s, an independent revolutionary force, calling itself the Pathet Lao (literally,

"Lao Nation"), established its headquarters in the small village of Vieng Xai, a town between Xam Neua and Xam Tai, essentially splitting Laos into two governing authorities: the Pathet Lao in northeastern Laos (Houaphan and Phongsali Provinces), and the Royal Lao Government that held the Mekong Basin.

The Pathet Lao headquarters remained in Vieng Xai for twenty-two years, eleven of them under bombardment, until gaining full political power in Laos and relocating to far-more-accessible Vientiane in 1975. Today, Vieng Xai is open to any tourist eager for a Lao history lesson.

The Vietnamese declared independence from France in 1954, exacerbating the regional tensions, and in the early 1960s, the United States became militarily involved in the larger conflict, concerned about the "spread of communism" and determined to support its allies in the region. Violence spread, military coups were attempted, and the region exploded into what the Lao call "The American War." Laos's eastern Houaphan Province, which borders both China and North Vietnam, now became the target, along with much of the rest of eastern Laos, of the most nightmarish military interventions of modern times.

Cluster-bomb casings repurposed into an elevated onion garden out of range of animals.

The Plain of Jars in old Muang Phuan contains multiple sites of 2,500-year-old carved stone jars of uncertain origin.

While Laos declared itself "neutral" to hostilities in the Vietnam War, its porous land border blurred the lines of the enemies. Between 1964 and 1973, the United States launched a "secret war" on Laos to "stem the flow of communism"—a war so secret not even the U.S. Congress was told. Houaphan Province, along with its western neighbor Xieng Khouang Province and the entire eastern spine of Laos to its southern border, was destroyed in a bombing campaign designed to stop the "Ho Chi Minh Trail"—that is, the flow of soldiers, weapons, and support from China that were to be used in Vietnam against U.S.-led forces.

Over two million tons of bombs were dropped on Laos's population of four million, more than had been dropped in the entire European theatre during World War Two. This is the equivalent of dropping one planeload of bombs each and every eight minutes for nine years, some ten times the weight of the entire Lao population. This remote jungle region was carpeted with cluster bombs, pummeled with larger bombs, sprayed with defoliant, and made the target of the most violent modern war effort against any people anywhere.

The Xam Tai District of Houaphan Province was not carpet bombed with cluster munitions to the degree of other Houaphan districts or its neighboring province, Xieng Khouang; by virtue of isolation and a southeastern orientation, the Ho Chi Minh Trail flowed to the west of this corner of Houaphan. Those districts to the west, however, that were the recipient of American cluster bombs, today still face the challenge of dealing with the 30 percent of these munitions that did not detonate upon ground contact, many of which are still explosive when they encounter a twenty-first-century pickax, a working plow, or a curious child.

The Xam Tai District was bombed with other munitions, however, and the devastation was thorough. But with the cessation of the war in 1974, the nightmare of explosions more or less ended. (That said, every type of bomb has a failure rate, and all regions of Laos that were bombed are still plagued with unexploded ordnance.)

In 1975, the Pathet Lao overthrew its oppressors as the U.S. withdrew from its untenable mission, and the Lao People's Democratic Republic was consolidated. And left in ruins.

At the cessation of bombing, not one structure in Xam Neua was left intact.

Upon independence, Laos was branded a "communist regime" by the United States and the West, although Laos, a nation with long-held Buddhist sentiment, over a hundred ethnic groups, no cash, and few resources, refers to itself as "Democratic Socialist." Until 2004, it remained despised on the United States' No-Trade List, sharing company with only the terrorist states of Libya and North Korea.

In much of eastern Laos after the war, civilization's evidence had to be literally rebuilt by this young government that had been born from military conflict but had few significant resources or trusted allies. The Pathet Lao did not put much trust in the Chinese, Russians, or Vietnamese; these governments were, and are still today, more aligned with serving their own people's economic and political needs. Rather, the Lao would need to unify and rebuild without the vast investment of resources of the industrialized world.

So Laos, with a new government, a destroyed infrastructure, few accessible resources, and without substantial outside investors, sealed its borders in 1974 and remained in isolation, effectively building relationships with the wide array of ethnic groups in Laos (some of whom did not support the Pathet Lao in its battle for independence); then, more slowly, it began to rebuild its relationships with its neighbors, especially modern Thailand, which shares its Buddhist traditions. Today, Thailand is Laos's largest trading partner, and Thai soap operas, potato chips, and skin-whitening lotion are readily available, even in remote villages.

This isolation in the 1970s and 1980s had an interesting side benefit for handcrafted textiles: it nourished the need for locals to maintain, and even reinvigorate, their textile traditions. We'll revisit this in Chapter 15: "Sinh and Other Daily-Use Textiles."

In 1986, Laos finally began to open its borders to allow a slow trickle of international tourists. With minimal accommodation and transportation infrastructure, most travelers have been, and are still, perceived as "brave" to endure the inconveniences and unpredictability of an underdeveloped tourist industry. But slowly the roads are being surfaced, and tourism companies are now able to entice both adventurers who wish to go further afield and those who prefer to be pampered.

Today, the modern city and capital of Vientiane is a flurry of cars and air-conditioned businesses. Its Mekong riverfront has been rebuilt to withstand the predictable floods; construction is rampant. The northern city of Luang Prabang, a World Heritage Site left unbombed, has taken a swift turn to capitalism with hotels and restaurants to suit even the most affluent. Its stunning fourteenth-century temples and colorful night market deservedly attract a worldwide audience. The rugged and rapidly developing city of Phonsavan, Xieng Khouang Province's capital, seeks to be a springboard to the tourist-appealing, mysterious Plain of Jars. In 2007, Phonsavan was a dusty outpost; in 2016, it's a dusty, modern city. Airports are now operating regular flights out of seven cities; Xam Neua is supposed to join their ranks soon.

While tourists are free to go almost anywhere, most cling together on a couple of well-defined, western-convenient "banana-pancake" routes. We always laugh at how so many people venture to such a far and different world only to spend time with people just like themselves. Still, I am also amazed at how one can walk for fifteen minutes from just about any major tourist spot and find a world apart from the bustle.

The provincial capital of Xam Neua has perhaps doubled in size since we first visited in 2006. The riverbanks are now constrained in an attractive stone-lined channel. New schools, boulevards, parks, and several massive government buildings have recently been constructed. There's an internet café, and our Xam Neua friends can now be found on Facebook. Last year, we saw Xam Neua's first car taxi. Children clog streets as they go to and from school. Someone with a blender now even sits on the street corner selling banana-mango smoothies.

Lots of hope. Lots of change.

CHAPTER EIGHT

# Yiim of Xam Tai

The home next to Tiip's house has five looms underneath, all vacant save the one in the middle. The ceiling height under this home is only about five and a half feet (1.8 m) high, so Maren, Malaithong, photographer Joe Coca, and I have to crouch as we approach the lone weaver and her loom.

"Sabaidee," Maren says to the young woman. "May we see what you are weaving?"

The young woman whispers a quick "Sabaidee" and raises her right hand over her mouth to cover a nervous laugh. With her left hand, she covers the row of weft she is working on. Although school had gotten out several hours earlier, she is still dressed in her school uniform—a plain white blouse and dark blue sinh with a white border at the hem.

Malaithong translates Maren's words, and the young woman giggles again and pulls her left hand back to display her deft finger-work on the current project. Although we could only view a small section of the back side of a textile, we could see that she was creating an ornate silk temple cloth, a phaa biang, with red ground colors (warp and weft) behind a gold-edged "diamonds of flowers" motif.

"My name is Maren." Maren says slowly in English. "What is your name?" Maren asks, echoing the only sure English words taught to every Lao child in school.

The young woman smiles, hunches her shoulders a little, and

Yiim at her loom. At right, a love token with the box of naga pattern.

looks shyly at the ground. "Yiim" she whispers faintly.

"Glad to meet you, Yiim" Maren says quietly. "My name is … Ma-ren."

Yiim tries to hide her smile again behind her hand, but keeps her eyes on her shoes. The rattle of camera gear lifts her eyes, and Yiim suddenly turns to Malaithong and rattles off a furtive, though still nearly silent, plea. Malaithong nods and Yiim quickly excuses herself with a quick "sabaidee" with her hands and dashes out from under the home and around a far corner.

"She wishes to wear something better for the photo," Malaithong confirms. In two minutes, Yiim is back, now dressed in a loose-fitting team-emblazoned track suit. Maren looks at me with a "teenagers-and-their-fashions" grin.

Yiim is fifteen years old, and after a bit of cajoling by Maren and Malaithong, she opens up that she began weaving silk under her mother's guidance at age eight. The first pieces she wove were what the locals call "love tokens." In Lao, "love tokens" are called *phaa kan mon*, which Cheesman translates as "auspicious cloths." These are small handkerchief-sized silks about 8 inches by x 8 inches (20 cm x 20 cm) that contain one full design element. Tradition holds that these textiles would be woven by young women to impress potential suitors, and potential mothers-in-laws. A well-woven love token would be the sign of a skilled woman who can earn a living and help manage a household. More pragmatically, each "love token" requires only a small investment of silk, making them excellent "starter-sized" pieces for the young girls who show the patience and desire to work the loom.

At ten years old, Yiim graduated to weaving larger phaa biang, a woman's shoulder-cloth, such as what is on her loom right now. "This one my parents will sell in the market," she tells us proudly, although still at a whisper.

At age ten, Yiim had learned from her mother how to spin cotton, but, as Maren and I already know, cotton textiles do not earn as much for the weaver in the marketplace. Silk weaving yields a better return on one's time.

Yiim tells us that all the women in her family weave, which explains the row of looms.

She shyly agrees that she likes to weave, and dedicates about three hours a day to the task. She also attends middle school and has daily homework, so she is busy almost all of the day. She admits that not all of her friends like to, or even can, weave. But she likes the quiet finger work and watching the textile grow under her patient direction. She expects she will continue to weave as an adult.

Her dream job once out of high school? "To work for the government. I want to have an office job."

"One last question," Maren smiles. "And this one is tough: What is your favorite color?"

Yiim smiles after Malaithong translates. She glances at her textile, then up at Maren. "Red, of course," and she raises her hand to conceal her laugh.

CHAPTER NINE

# Entering the Twenty-First Century

For those who have grown up with a comfortable "first world" standard of living, the first experiences with rural travel in an "underdeveloped" nation can be shocking, and counter to expectations.

Laos creates two different rattles in visitors.

First, it's so easy to think: "So many people seem to have so little and so many homes, especially in the rural areas, look so…well…ramshackle. Kitchens are smoky fires set outside the back door, and toilets may be what you do for yourself in the woods. Naked young children run amok and the water buffalo drags the wooden plow through the rice paddies, much as it must have been for centuries…."

And then: From the depths of the shoulder bag of the petite old lady next to you comes a chime, and she whips out her iPhone 6 and chirps a sharp "'ello?" Yes, actually so. "'ello" is how most every cell phone is answered, regardless of the speaker's language.

Or perhaps you'll be invited to sing karaoke along with the village headman's new digital machine, powered by the Dutch-installed solar panels located behind the pigsty. Don't know any Lao songs? No problem ("Bo pen-yang!") "We have 'Hotel California,' or maybe some Phil Collins?"

Or perhaps, escaping the blazing midafternoon heat, you accept an invitation to sit under an elder's home, and you're suddenly offered a cold beer, on ice. Every village in every remote corner—and that village might be a two-day walk from the nearest road—will have Beer Lao, the delicious national lager, available in 640 ml. bottles.

Opposite: The new bridge over the Nam Xam at Xam Tai will connect the villages on the other side of the river year round. Above: Beer Lao is made and sold throughout Laos, and consumed with national pride by all.

You note that each room in the simple, clean guesthouse has a throne-style flush toilet, an on-demand hot water shower and, for $2 more per day, air-conditioning.

So, at the risk of diminishing that wonderful, personal feeling of being away and remote that Maren, the kids, and I sometimes nurture in our hearts and tales, here are some modern truths:

Wireless phone service is everywhere, and cell phone costs are minimal to allow people with little means to gain access to the technology. This has greatly reduced the isolation of those who live in areas with no (or perhaps seasonal) road access. A business transaction that a few years ago may have taken days of walking may now take only a few seconds. The modern globe, it turns out, doesn't have corners.

With wireless phone comes internet access. We now Facebook our Lao friends who speak English, and many locals, young and old, sport new iPhones. Reception is excellent; ask your guesthouse host for the wi-fi password.

The advent of trustworthy electricity changes everything. Complete dependability has allowed wealthier locals and guesthouses to recently begin to invest in refrigerators, laundry machines, television, blenders, and more.

Even small villages not connected to the power grid have low-wattage electricity. Solar panels and small river-driven propeller generators, often afforded thanks to foreign aid micro-projects, have gained almost every home a fluorescent bulb for evening light. These extended hours have dramatically changed post-dinner routines and many take advantage of the evening hours to earn or learn.

The last few years have seen an increase in dry farming and plantation-style farming that is backed by outside corporate interests. Many hillsides are burned and then seeded with corn, which in turn is sold as animal feed in Vietnam, creating a significant problem with erosion and nutrient depletion. Chinese-owned banana plantations are encroaching, bringing with them commercial fertilizers and large-scale pesticide use. And, as mentioned earlier, Xam Tai's elevation grants it the status of being

Rock weirs channel the current past small propeller generators for the town's electrical needs.

a hydroelectric battery; this construction is and will continue to bring in Chinese and Vietnamese workers, and assists in developing a basic infrastructure of roads, schools, guesthouses, access to the electric grid, and more.

Textile creation, and particularly the role of the weaver herself, is, for many, the only means that a family may have of acquiring cash beyond selling a bit of extra produce or foraged materials, and thus the time invested in weaving for pay is foundational for the home economics of the region. Earning a living by weaving is considered by the communities to be a sure, honorable way of helping a family afford a healthy

From top left: Creative checkerboard. Souksakone's guest house and current remodel. Girls practicing traditional dance for a school project. Father with his children in Xam Tai.

way forward. Assuming, of course, that the individual has the patience, dexterity, and intelligence to be a quality weaver. We're told that pay is comparable to a government worker or shopkeeper.

This lends the region a unique feature: much of the regional economy centers on activities and business performed by women. Perhaps that is why business in Xam Tai is so relationship-based, and why the status of women in the community is so high.

Perhaps "Mom's weaving a living at the loom" is also why we will more often see fathers physically caring for their children than we may see in other regions. As noted before, the Lao Loum people are traditionally matrilineal, reinforcing the respected and often empowered role of the woman within the culture.

In Xam Tai, as elsewhere in Houaphan Province, kids appear healthy and curious. Markets and gardens are full of delicious food. Basic costs are low. Elders and youngsters are cared for and family units remain strong, at least from our perspective as visitors.

Above and opposite: Cell phones are as popular in Laos as in the United States.

"Underdeveloped," is not "old-timey" or "backwards." Nor is it indicative of a lack of intelligence or drive. It is more that the citizens are just now gaining access to the opportunities and gadgetry that we have cultivated in the West. Also, and most particularly in Xam Tai, the people still feel the profound weight of cultural tradition. They have something special, unique, enduring. And they know it.

And then there's Rattle #2:

"The people, both those who seem to have some and those who have so very little, are extraordinarily friendly, giving, and gracious."

In Laos, and particularly in Xam Tai and neighboring Meung Kuan Districts, if you carry an open smile, relationships will open as well. So many strangers over our years of visits have given generously of their time and their company. Indeed, some of these strangers have become good friends.

Several factors account for the gentle and accessible warmth:

Many of the people are steeped in Buddhist traditions, and seem more attached to the present moment than people in the West. A "live and let live" attitude pervades. Others are steeped in traditions of animism, which grants special attention to the role of relationships, whether over the generations or between modern strangers. To separate the corporeal from the spiritual is to unwind a duality.

Cooperative politics and economics have been central to the stability of the region for centuries. We can see this in the traditional political construct of the muang. We see it today in the cooperative nature of the silk industry and economy.

Family is central to the social unit, and "family" can be a broader arrangement than we might expect in the West. Families often make no distinction between a son and a nephew, or a mother and aunt. Grandparents are often primary caretakers for small children. Our friend Malaithong is raising her niece, Nana, as her own child. Why? Because Nana is her own child.

There is, especially in smaller villages, a sense that all are working toward a common good. Perhaps that is because, given a history of poverty and challenge, working together actually yielded better results, whether the measure was in kilos of rice or keeping the local peace. In our experience, if (okay, when) a village adult saw Ari or Zall doing something stupid, like goofing around the public water source or trying to balance on an unstable fence, that local would speak to our kids as if he or she were the parent. Granted, they're admonishing in Lao, but it is equally persuasive.

Finally, and we don't quite get it either, there just appears to be a bit of magic in rural Laos, and Xam Tai in particular. As I commented before, the pressure valve has released just a little more tension from the air. The breeze is just a little more soft-hearted. The rhythm of each unfolding day seems more treasured, and more of a treasure.

Call it a pervasive sense of general well-being.

However, as you'll learn, the secret may lie in the looms and traditions, as we'll see in Chapter 14: "Weaving as Well-Being."

The silk artists of Xam Tai do have some twenty-first-century challenges to negotiate if they wish to survive. Can a market for their weaving be sustained? Will it follow a path that is determined solely by economics, or can the act of weaving and the textiles themselves remain a vital cultural marker, a source of spirit and pride? As the generations become more globally aware and gain access to information and markets, will textile creation satisfy a social and cultural need? Will traditional motifs and designs remain relevant, or will they transform to meet the pull of a distant market? Will the future generations of weavers find meaning and vitality in weaving as other opportunities—perhaps a college education—become accessible?

We have already witnessed, in our few years, a sure change in what is being woven. The market now seems to be chasing the rising Lao middle class, especially those in the wealthier urban markets, and is less focused on the up-and-down tourist market.

The cold truth is that artists who need to earn a living with their efforts must follow the market. Where will our new and globally-connected modern market take them? Where will these incredible skills and talents trend?

Finally, a quick word on twenty-first-century silk economics. Silk is a valued commodity worldwide, and the price and availability relies on global factors. Between 2013 and 2015 alone, the cost of Lao raw silk doubled. Makers of lingerie and shirts and ties are eager to generate more silk, and factories for silk production, especially in powerhouse economies like China, Vietnam, or Thailand, are expanding to meet demand. Such inflation and global pressure poses an economic, and thus cultural, challenge to the small-village sericulturist, and the gifted hand-reeler, and the traditional dye artist, and the individual weaver who together, for millennia, have generated the textiles of the region.

However, the twenty-first-century textile artists in Xam Tai are neither naïve nor helpless. They recognize that their deliberate efforts and attention to address these challenges are and will continue to be essential as they negotiate a path into the future that can both retain their cultural integrity as creative traditional artists, but also meet the needs of a dynamic, evolving marketplace.

CHAPTER TEN

# Mai of Xam Tai

Walking up Xam Tai's back road from Yiim's home, we find another weaver, an older woman we've seen many times but do not know by name. Her loom makes a little more clatter than we normally hear, and we notice that there is no vertical template pattern strung across the warp strings.

"Sabaidee," Maren beckons, and the woman glances up quickly, gives a quick smile, and returns her eyes immediately to the task of her hands.

She is weaving indigo-dyed handspun cotton into a popular style of sinh. We tend not to see a lot of cotton weaving in Xam Tai; as mentioned earlier, silk weaving in today's economics is more favorable to a weaver's time. Previous to this generation, however, cotton was raised and woven extensively for practical daily-wear clothing, and thus we still find some people engaged in the art of spinning and weaving cotton.

The extra clicks are due to a second warp system she has installed onto her loom that allows her to weave supplemental decorative stripes of white as the regular indigo-dyed warp and weft threads are woven. The pattern is very traditional.

The woman continues her focused weaving. Her loom

Mai weaving a handspun cotton indigo-dyed skirt. Opposite: She takes a quick break from weaving.

has the standard two heddles for plain weave, each controlled by a foot treadle. Behind this pair of heddles is an additional set of four heddles (each controlled by other foot treadles, hence the extra clicks and clacks). Her feet seem as busy as her arms as she lifts sets of threads and slides her shuttle back and forth.

She stops after a few moments and turns toward us with a warm smile. "Sabaidee," she says quietly, hands pressed under her chin. We all return the gesture.

Malaithong knows the woman from her youth, and the two of them share a moment of untranslated words as they hold each other's hands.

"Mai says she has seen you many times, and she is glad you have stopped by her home." In fact, she is one of the women who regularly joins us at Phout's home; we have purchased several textiles from her over the years. Mai smiles brightly and looks directly into our eyes as Malaithong translates.

"I am now seventy-five years old," she tells us. "I have seen many changes here in Xam Tai, but I still spend much of my time at the loom. I find it relaxing; it keeps me busy." Her time also is providing some beautiful and practical apparel for her family, or perhaps for the market.

Mai has sat at her loom almost every day for more than sixty-five years, and she acknowledges that she is adept with both cotton and silk. She has planted, picked, ginned, carded, dyed, and woven cotton. She also raises silkworms and has been responsible for some of the beautiful silk ceremonial cloths our business seeks. She shrugs as if such talent and dedication is the norm.

She tells us proudly that she is the mother of four boys and four girls, and that she taught all of her daughters to weave, and also all of her granddaughters. All of her children now "work in the office," an acknowledgment that they earn a steady wage, and are not subsistence farmers. Several pursued a college education, and others gained skills through the army.

We smile with the translation, and Mai gently leans forward towards us and nods several times.

She then turns back to face her loom and picks up the richly-patinaed shuttle with her left hand. Her right foot pushes down on a treadle and one of the loom's supplemental heddles clicks upward. She slides the shuttle through the created shed to her right hand; her feet do a quick shift, and there are more clicks as one heddle lowers and another rises. Mai's face tightens with concentration.

We watch and listen for another minute. Maren finally nods and presses her hands together under her chin as a "Thank you," and we all rise to continue our walk. Mai smiles and nods gently once more, but keeps her hands moving and her eyes focused on the loom straight in front of her.

A young Buddhist monk carves a drum for the village's new temple.

The challenge is, of course, that both the people studying (including Maren, me, and now you, the reader) and the people being studied are just that: living, dynamic people. We are immersed in a complexity of relationships that affect our thoughts, actions, and perceptions. Who we are at the beginning of our life is not necessarily who we are at the end, and certainly who one's great-grandparents were has little effect in our modern times as to who the great-grandchildren will define themselves to be. We are complex tapestries, and not the added sum of the threads.

Here is a selection of human relationship-caused complexities cited by researchers in our bibliography who are trying to untangle this knot of relationships that has been getting more snarled in each of some 400 generations:

Ethnic self-identification may change for an individual, family, or entire clan by virtue of adopting another's ways. For example, in Xam Tai District, both Tai Daeng people, who are traditionally animist, and Lao Loum people, who are traditionally Buddhist, share effort in the local economy; they often intermarry. However, if a person of Tai Daeng heritage starts practicing Buddhist ways, she may, or may not, now refer to herself as "Lao Loum."

Recent arrivals, whether in the mountains of Laos or in the halls on Ellis Island, generally seek to be accepted by the local, dominant group, and members of persecuted or immigrant ethnic groups often change their self-recognized ethnic identity in order to thrive. The Khmu Ou of Houaphan Province have largely adopted the habitat, language, and clothing style of the larger Tai Daeng ethnic group. Maren's grandfather, arriving in America as a Danish immigrant, changed his last name from "Bak" to "Beck" to be more readily accepted. At what point is cultural identity lost? When the last words of the language are spoken? When the elders no longer tell their ancestors' stories?

Many smaller ethnic groups did not (and still do not) have written language; their traditions are oral. Upon resettling, these groups often have had to absorb the language of the regional power in order to participate in regional economics. In the ages of the muangs, some regional leaders required citizens to adopt culturally-identifying garments and practices in order to harness the power of political unity, regardless of the traditional ethnicity of an individual. People, perhaps by choice and perhaps by coercion, may change ethnic identity in order to meet the desires of the political state or the pragmatic assurance that one's family is safe and fed.

Pronunciations, dialects, and accents vary, and both locals and anthropologists often have a tough time separating the "Lu" from the "Lue," the "Tai" from the "Tay," and the "Kho Chapo Nyai" from the "Kho Chapo Noy." Then complicate the situation with the adage that researchers most readily hear what they expect or want to hear. Information is only as mistake-free as both your source, and the clear understanding of your source.

There are discrepancies between autonyms—what a group calls itself, and exonyms—what others call the group. Further, some people self-describe their (or another's) ethnic group using loconyms, identifying someone by a nearby natural feature. The abstraction of one's genetic history wrapped in a DNA strand is not a locally-valued characteristic.

From 1954 to1975 the Lao government divided its citizens into three categories: Lao Loum (lowlanders, living at 200–400 meters altitude), Lao Theung (dwellers at 300–900 meters), and Lao Soung (dwellers at 800–1600 meters). Thus, a person educated in this era may call herself "Lao Loum" simply by virtue of the elevation of her home.

Categorization has political implications; the degree of a group's recognized status grants the power of the group's political voice. An unrecognized minority has no voice, whereas a coalition of sub-groups may find a unifying ethnic identity to create a representative voice of a hundred thousand. With recognition comes organization, and with organization comes clout. Bottom line: regional politics plays a substantive role in ethnic identification.

Beyond politics, regional ethnic biases and prejudices play a role in self-identification. In the Lao-Tai language family, the root form "*kha*" refers to slavery, and several distinct groups—the Kh'mu, Katu, and others—have an ethnic marker of having once been a "slave class." Such subtleties, I can only imagine, may still play an inherited role between some groups in some areas.

And here are a few things that Maren and I, and I'm certain many others, have encountered when doing "field research".

People often agree with a statement we are trying to verify out of friendliness, respect, or confusion. It's far more tactful to agree with a nod and a smile than to articulate a counter-truth or confess to ignorance or lack of understanding. To help counter this, we've learned not to lead by asking "Is this the siho motif?" but rather "What motif is this?" Not that this necessarily clears up any confusion.

A local can say "yes, yes, yes" ("*chou, chou, chou*") when she may mean any of:

a) "Yes, I agree with the content of what you are saying",

b) "Yes, I understand what you are saying, but I am neither agreeing nor disagree-

The old floating bamboo bridge was the only link for people and motorcycles crossing the Nam Xam. It was replaced with a concrete bridge in 2014.

ing",

c) "Yes, the sound of the words is entering my ears", or

d) "Yes, I will smile and nod and this will all pass shortly."

Nuance and detail are easily lost when language is translated through a third party. Not that this makes a relationship any less enjoyable or satisfying; it just doesn't fill a book with confident facts.

Translators are often guides, and guides may have multiple agendas. Perhaps the guide seeks to gain a personal economic benefit; perhaps he has a political agenda; or perhaps she is focused on facilitating "friendliness" more than translating accurately.

Some people will say almost anything if they think it will gain a sale.

The academic effort to categorize and subdivide finds its limit in the complex and dynamic nature of the inevitable human relationships that create the fabric of our lives and the lives or those who came before us. Despite a yearning for clarity, certain desired facts—especially those shaped by our interactions with each other—lend themselves to neither purity nor conclusiveness.

That said, academics do their best.

By analyzing language forms, ethno-lin-

Young women in their school uniforms hurry to class.

guists can "watch" the expansions and migrations of portions of the population as they move southward. Migrating groups quickly become detached from the old order and thus languages and other identifying cultural attributes develop separately. Some groups come to recognize Buddhism as a source of tradition and ethic. Other groups, especially those that remained more isolated, retained their traditions of animism.

At every step of the way, differing traditions and ethnic groups intermingled, sometimes in peace and sometimes in conflict. Hidden within these interactions is the fact that comingling groups often intermarried and conducted trade with each other. Thus, every migration leaves some behind, usually those who most adopted the ways of the dominant culture. Thus, not only are the bloodlines of ethnicity made impossible to trace over time, but so are the sources of the customs and traditions of any particular people. Indeed, traces of the original Lao-Tai culture can be found from India's mountains to Indonesia's islands.

Also, as these various regional ethnic groups intersect, certain textile traditions, whether a spiritual motif or preferred dye color, may be "borrowed" and merged with another's traditions. There is no one tradition, nor is there an authority to keep track of who started what. And there is no available archaeological-style evidence to trace motifs and styles to a beginning, as textiles themselves have a shelf life that pales in comparison to the age of the traditions.

Additionally, the age of being able to identify peoples' ethnicity by their clothing,

The recently-gilded Buddhist temple on the left rises from the trees above Xam Tai.

headdress, housing type, or other marker in Laos is rapidly fading, and often misleading. A woman's skirt may be an identifying characteristic (and fashion statement), but virtually everyone has access to modern markets where western and Chinese factory-made clothing and goods are sold—some even pre-printed with "ethnic designs"—and western dress, outside of a women's sinh, is now standard wear for both men and women.

That, and the cheerful Lao Loum shopkeeper is eager to sell the Tai Daeng-style sinh woven by the Tai Neua woman to the Khamu customer. Indeed, local economics makes for good neighbors.

## Ethnic Groups

Laos's Houaphan Province is home to a quarter million people who fall into sixteen government-recognized ethnic groups: Khamu, Xinh Mun, Khang, Phuan, Tai Dam, Tai Khao, Tai Neua, Tai Souei, Tai Daeng, Tai Add, Tai Pua, Hmong, Yao, Haw, Phunoi, as well as Laos's dominant group (and here we'll use the ethnic title preferred in Xam Tai), the Lao Loum. Ethnic Lao Loum people, who comprise 60 percent of Laos's total population (the other 40 percent comprising the other 130-plus minority groups) may also refer to themselves as Lao-Tai, Lao, Phou Lao, or Tai Lao.

Of Houaphan's sixteen ethnic groups, the Hmong, Yao, Tai Dam, Tai Daeng, Tai Khao, Tai Neua, and Lao Loum all have traditions of distinct textile creation that persist today. While the Hmong and Yao work almost exclusively with hemp, cotton, and now synthetic textiles, and this primarily in Houaphan's northern Muang Et District, the Tai groups and the Lao Loum in Xam Tai District work almost exclusively with silk, cotton, and their synthetic substitutes.

The Lao Loum and Tai Daeng of this region have uniquely bonded in an effort to be mutually successful. Despite differing fundamental traditional belief systems—the Lao Loum emerging from the tradition of Theravada Buddhism and the Tai Daeng from animism—a faith in the strength of cooperation has bonded the community at a level deeper than ethnic labels.

The Lao Loum and Tai Daeng cooperation in textile creation and textile use speaks to this spirit of mutual survival and support. It also speaks to a spiritual collaboration, as many ceremonies, such as Laos's unique Baci, have roots in both Buddhism and animism. Indeed, both the Lao Loum and Tai Daeng people in the region have a tradition of performing shamanic rituals for healing, placating spirits, and warding off evil spirits, and the regional traditions all incorporate textiles into ceremony.

So where does that leave us?

It leaves us in Houaphan's beautiful Xam Tai District, with hazy explanations regarding the development of regional textile traditions, and it leaves our western-trained personal desire for clarity and precision unsatisfied. It also generates a challenge to understand why this particular district has elevated the art of silk textile creation and tradition beyond what is found elsewhere in the world.

But we will hazard a guess. The tradition and cultural drive of textile art and industry in Xam Tai developed out of the unique slurry of circumstances and peoples particular to this remote region in the Annamite Mountains. This Spark of intense creativity and pride arises from a brew that includes:

• A mix of minority ethnicities whose mutual traditions and survival depended on stability and cooperation,

• A mix of world-paradigms, with the animist traditions of the Tai Daeng (and others) blending with Buddhist traditions of the Lao Loum,

• An isolated locale that was uniquely impacted by larger outside forces (from the north, east, south and west), with history at times granting stability and trade, and at other times forcing isolation and self-reliance.

• The reliance through the ages on women to steer the industry of silk-textile creation and the transmission of the cultural heritage embedded in the art (more on this later),

• Strong leadership from within. The leaders of today's silk textile activity in Xam Tai—the people who use their creative skills and business savvy to generate and manage the successful industry for all involved—are an intelligent, innovative, talented, resourceful group who are aware of the delicate balance required for their community's cultural and economic success.

The challenge of maintaining the inherent beauty and integrity of these various groups as the world consolidates brings pause to my breath. How rapidly the weaving arts of the world are being lost to the world of inexpensive, factory-made clothing. How many people have lost track of their ancestors, and their traditions, and their essential relationship with the flow of time and culture? What beauty and perspectives have been lost? In most places of the world, close cultural relationships are not necessarily balanced relationships, and history everywhere tells us that dom-

inant cultures tend to absorb subcultures, whether by force of arms or by virtue of raw pragmatism.

But Xam Tai? What an anomaly. Perhaps this small garden has found that soft spot on the balance, allowing tradition and modernity and expression and pragmatism to celebrate together and express a unique and tantalizing whole.

Like a fluid, we bend and blend as we flow from day to day and from generation to generation. We are raised and formed and colored and woven and worn, and this one life we each savor is textured by it all.

The beautiful Xam Tai valley in the dry season of March. The monsoon usually arrives in May, creating lush, emerald-green rice paddies.

CHAPTER TWELVE

# Lun and Bounkeo

Colors can enrich each other. Many fine silks have an eye-popping shimmer as differing warp and weft colors play off each other, whether in opposition or by complement. A brick red warp tussling with an algae-green weft can reflect an undulant, magical sheen—a sea of iridescence. Or, more subtly, a navy-blue warp teamed with a charcoal-indigo weft can radiate a royal, luxurious sparkle—a late evening's sky.

People, too, can enrich each other. Sometimes as opposites, the extrovert and the introvert. Sometimes as complements—two peas in a pod, as it were. Regardless, some couples seem to shimmer when they're together, their united selves greater than the two taken separately.

Lun and Bounkeo are such a couple. When apart, they are decent and kind and gentle; but when together, the air in the room sparks. Perhaps it seems all the sweeter because, in a country where affection and romance are rarely displayed, these round-faced middle-agers light up in each other's company, sharing sweet looks and laughs that lift everyone in their company.

Lun and Bounkeo leave you wanting to be in love.

"It is because Bounkeo is Tai Daeng," Phout teases, "And Lun is Lao Loum. They make a perfect balance." Everyone laughs, and Bounkeo and Lun share a warm glance.

The couple was introduced to our family on our second visit to Xam Tai, the first with Malaithong. Lun is, by some distant reach, Malaithong's cousin (who isn't?), and she is one of the renowned master dyers in the district. On that first visit, Lun took the time to show us the process for creating the region's rich red using lac, a secretion from a scale bug collected from tree limbs in the jungle. We also pawed through several dozen newly completed pieces she had retrieved from "her weavers," selecting what we believed to be the choicest textiles for our new-formed business.

Today, she has about fifty weavers who work under her direction, creating textiles to meet her expectations and the market's demand. Like several master-dyers in the district, Lun supplies both the silk she has dyed and the design template to the weaver, who then weaves the textile. Upon completion, the textile returns to Lun, who, along with her husband, Bounkeo, has the responsibility of getting the textile to the marketplace. (The relationship between master dyers contracting with weavers will be looked at more closely later.)

Lun is quiet and holds a modest reserve. The textiles she represents and the patterns she uses are intricate and complex, but still conservative and traditional, and they rely heavily on traditional Tai Daeng motifs. The bulk of her weavers are located "off towards Bounkeo's home village"—a village that is historically Tai Daeng—which might explain her textiles' dominant symbology. Her specialty is the phaa biang textiles, full-length silks decorated from end to end with twisting motifs created from the discontinuous supplemental weft style of Lao weaving. Her color palette, like all the master-dyers, is broad and relies on rich reds and golds, but Lun also sprinkles in a touch of lighter, non-jewel-tone hues, some that approach pastel.

Lun's husband, Bounkeo, one of the few men we've met who is intimately involved in the textile world, helps facilitate the coor-

Bounkeo and Lun outside their home in Xam Tai. Lun designed and dyed the silk for her shoulder cloth.

dination of resources, weavers, and the marketplace; he has also been an important cultural translator—not just for Maren and me, but also for academics visiting the region. In addition to his textile business responsibilities, Bounkeo is also responsible for farming his family's rice fields. He is a kind, cheerful man: it was he who first invited fifteen-year-old Ari to share a beer and play a game of petanque. On every visit, Bounkeo is still first to inquire about our boys.

Lun holding her new granddaughter. Opposite: Lun's design and natural dyes spark this ceremonial wedding blanket with saang hong and khon buhan motifs.

Both Lun and Bounkeo were born in small villages in Xam Tai District. Lun was raised in a Lao Loum village with six brothers and sisters, and she started weaving and dyeing both cotton and silk at age ten under the direction of her mother and grandmother.

Bounkeo was raised in a Tai Daeng village with seven brothers and sisters, and even though both his father and grandfather were once village chiefs, he was expected to work in the rice fields like everyone else. Perhaps, Bounkeo now laughs, he was expected to work even a little harder.

The couple met while attending secondary school in Xam Tai, but Bounkeo had to leave school to make sure his family could make ends meet. He stayed in Xam Tai, however, and opened a business selling clothes, sweets, and cooking utensils. Apparently, Lun spent a lot of time "shopping" at his store.

They married in 1986, and had four sons in quick succession. As a young parent, Lun remembers having to purchase factory-spun Vietnamese cotton (she herself did not learn to spin), which she dyed and wove to meet her family's needs.

It was not until 1993 that she turned to silk and the emerging business opportunity of weaving for an outside market. She reeled and dyed the silk in her community's tradition, and then used her old pattern-templates—the type with bamboo memory sticks—to weave traditional phaa biang ceremonial cloths. A businessman from Luang Prabang was drawn to her work, providing her first contact for distributing her own textiles to the larger marketplace.

With help from her friend Souksakone, whom you will meet later, Lun "learned how to find the market"; in 1995 she started to contract other weavers to work with her dyed silk and template designs to produce textiles for the emerging tourist markets in Luang Prabang and Vientiane.

Twenty years later, Lun and Bounkeo work with more than four dozen weavers, many of whom continue to live in their small traditional villages, but who, through their weaving work, can gain access to the cash economy.

Both Lun and Bounkeo speak openly about the need to maintain their traditional patterns and methods. Both believe their adherence to the natural methods will generate greater benefits in the long run, and they bemoan the fact that today so many textile creators—and the market itself—are surrendering to the ease and benefits of chemical dyes, factory-reeled silk, acrylic fibers, and mass-produced clothing.

"Keeping our expertise with the natural processes makes us unusual," Bounkeo explains. "It is what makes sure that Xam Tai textiles continue to be the very best—that they are authentic, tomasat (natural) textiles."

Lun admits she worries about the dedication of the next generation. None of her children are interested in textiles (granted, they are all boys), and she questions whether the next generation will have the drive and patience to keep the art alive.

# three. Textiles in Village Life

*Relationships are necessarily messy; they force us to not be static. They force us to evolve and become, over time, more ourselves.*

*They shape, nurture, and surprise. They can defeat.*

*Like cultures stumbling over each other for century after century, we too stumble into our friends and acquaintances for years and years, even generations.*

*How we steer in the world of our relationships—what we take, what we leave, how we act and whom we engage—shapes who we are; our relationships create our very unique selves.*

*Ultimately, we are whom we meet.*

CHAPTER THIRTEEN

# Me Tau Lu of Ban Tao

The elderly woman, intently concentrating on the narrow weaving set on the full frame loom in front of her, chews on her lips as her thin, brittle fingers deliberately tie the supplemental colors into a row of silk weft. Her hands, knuckles swollen with arthritis, reach automatically for the shuttle and she deftly taps the shuttle between the warp threads, adding another silk-thin length to the narrow skirt border she is weaving. Upon completion, the five-inch-wide (13 cm) cloth will be sewn onto the bottom of a sinh for colorful decoration and as protection of the larger skirt body.

She glances at our faces briefly, and I hold up my small camera with raised eyebrows in a silent appeal for permission to film her. She gives a quick nod, sharpens her posture, and returns to the methodical and creative task of turning silk thread into beauty and spirit. I push the start button and begin to archive her talent.

She licks her lips and sets a firm and consistent pace as the camera studies her deliberate and smooth motions. Her deep, moist eyes measure every finger's movement.

The woman is working with silk raised in her village, Ban Tao, which is renowned for its sericulture. Her pattern template (*khao nyeung*), the web of "instructions" that assures every weft line is accurately formed, is made of a coarser string than usual, no doubt because it is easier to feel and manipulate with her worn fingers. The design requires surprisingly intricate finger motions in inserting the supplemental weft colors, and the shapes of the textile's woven motifs are knife-edge precise.

She works her fingers in an even rhythm. Perhaps her fingers are a little slower than those of a nimble twenty-year-old, but her measured precision, molded by eighty years of practice, reveals an adept efficiency that is a pleasure to watch. She weaves for three minutes in focused silence as I film her from a variety of angles and zoom in on her patient finger work.

I click off the camera and casually bow my head with my hands together under my chin as a "Thank you."

"She is the oldest woman in the village." Malaithong's voice surprises us—she had been visiting an elderly aunt down the road and had crept up on us. Malaithong nods with a formal "Sabaidee" toward Me Tau Lu, who smiles and nods herself. "I have known this woman over forty years," Malaithong continues. "Her name is Lu, and we call her Me Tau Lu, Grandmother Lu."

Malaithong turns and asks a question of Me Tau Lu. The elder stops her concentration, smiles toothlessly at us, and returns a paragraph of words.

"She says she is nearly ninety year old," Malaithong translates. "She does not know exactly how old, but she can remember back longer than anyone else in Ban Tao. She wonders if you would like to see a piece she has finished. Perhaps you would like to buy it?"

"Of course we would like to see your finished piece," Maren answers. The elder turns to a young boy who has been watching and gives a sharp direction. He dashes off, only to appear a moment later with a tidily folded sinh held flat in his hands.

Through Malaithong, we learn that this skirt had been made a few years ago, back when her fingers were more nimble and her

Opposite: Me Tau Lu in 2016. Previous page: A handspun cotton blanket from Muang Kuan.

eyesight sharper. Given the sinh's size and intricacy, it must have taken her two or more months to weave.

She stands up from her worn loom bench and takes the fabric from the boy's outstretched arms. She shuffles into the sunshine and, after straightening her posture, she wraps the skirt tightly across her belly to show off the intricate pattern.

Indeed it is a stunning silk sinh. The pattern is of an older style showing vertical stripes, a less common skirt form. The central motif of her sinh is also less common: the crab, which lives (and is hunted) in the freshwater rivers.

"Did you spend your childhood here?" Maren asks through Malaithong.

"Yes," Me Tau Lu answers as she poses. "I was born in this village, and I raised my children and grandchildren and now their children here, too."

"What do you remember from your childhood?"

"I remember the French authorities when they visited us here. They came a couple of times. They walked down the street and shook our hands. I thought they were very kind—and tall, too."

"Do you remember the war?"

"Oh, yes. I remember the bombs and the sounds that they made. We had to move our home into some caves that are over that way," and she waves her hand toward the limestone hills.

"We worked the fields at night then, planting and harvesting the rice." Her voice is firm, and she looks directly at us as she speaks. "I remember quickly wrapping my baby onto my back and running to the cave when I heard the planes come. I had young children then. Now they are grown up and old, like me," she laughs. "Several of them now live in Vientiane, and one lives here in Ban Tao."

Maren eyes Me Tau Lu's skirt, still stretched across her waist, and says to the woman in Lao, "*Sinh, ngam lai*" (very beautiful). Me Tau Lu turns towards me, points to my camera and stiffens herself. She holds a firm face for the photo; smiles are reserved for present, shared moments, not moments frozen in time. I snap a shot.

She flips a quick few words to Mai, who smiles. "Me Tau Lu asks if you want to buy this sinh. It is for sale."

"Chou chou!" Maren blurts out, turning directly to the weaver. "Um...Me Tau Lu, *sinh todai*?" Skirt how much?

The elder offers Maren a grin and nods her head up and down. The two of them take perhaps fifteen seconds to agree to a price—

Me Tau Lu shows an unusual sinh with vertical stripes of crab motifs.

Maren does know her Lao numbers well.

Perhaps the price is just a little high for the going rate in the region, but, on the other hand, this silk carries a certain provenance, knowing it represents a culmination of a lifetime of skill and effort. Its very manifestation harbors an element of her precious uniqueness—her vital, relevant breath.

Each unique, handwoven textile does carry the spirit of its creator.

We pay the proud weaver in cash. She counts the bills carefully and folds them into the waistband at the top of her own faded sinh.

The woman looks directly at Maren and tosses out another line.

Malaithong laughs. "She wants to know if you want to see another skirt she wove."

### TWO YEARS LATER:

With Joe Coca in tow, we again visit Me Tau Lu at her home. We wake her from a midafternoon nap, but she quickly gathers herself and cheerfully answers our questions and poses for Joe. Her family crowds around to listen to us interview her more formally.

She agrees this year that she is ninety years old—the oldest person in Ban Tao—and for the first season in eighty-one years she is not weaving this year. Her eyes, she confirms, can no longer see the threads clearly. Her memory and engagement, however, are sharp and clear.

Me Tau Lu's first experience with textile creation was learning to spin cotton when she was nine years old; she was a daily cotton weaver, creating sinh by age eleven. She was not trusted with silk until she was eighteen years old, and her first woven silks were narrow-banded tiin sinh, decorative skirt borders.

She recalls being very poor when she was young, relying on the forest and river for their food. "I had to work very hard every day. There was no time, unlike today, for people to sit around. Now you can be lazy and still have a house and food," she chuckles.

As a young adult, she created all the textiles for her family. This included planting, harvesting, ginning, spinning, dyeing, and weaving the cotton, and raising, reeling, dyeing, and weaving the silk. She boasts of having made all the dyes the natural way in the old days.

Me Tau Lu has nine children: three daughters and six sons. All her daughters learned to weave and still weave today. She and her daughters first sold textiles just as post-war Laos was opening its doors to the world in 1995, and the change in cash flow helped her family very much. Now she celebrates the openness and freedom of the modern times, and relishes the new opportunities in education and travel available for her grandchildren and great-grandchildren.

"Do you have a special childhood memory you'd like to share?" asks Maren as a final question.

Me Tau Lu pauses for a moment. "I can't think of anything—we had to work so hard…I do remember a game we used to play. A kicking game with a nut from a tree."

Me Tau Lu and her daughter-in-law in front of their shared home.

A great-grandchild-aged kid who is sitting in the room laughs and reaches into his pocket and shows everyone his three polished brown chestnuts. He hands them to Me Tau Lu.

She looks at the child and smiles.

"Yes," she says. "We used to…" and she stops talking. She leans forward on her cushion and sets two chestnuts in front of her cross-legged feet, and the third one in front of Maren, perhaps two feet away. Without saying a thing, she nimbly flicks her foot forward, her toe striking the nut with a solid thwack. The nut flies across the linoleum floor and very precisely knocks Maren's chestnut aside.

The crowd gasps for a brief second—bulls-eye!

Everyone cheers and laughs at her perfect shot, and Me Tau Lu's smile, just for a moment, carries the glow of a young, proud girl.

CHAPTER FOURTEEN

# Weaving as Well-Being

While reserved and academic in their categorization of types and designs, textile scholars of this region are, when discussing the role of the weaver, prone to suddenly turn to metaphor and wax poetic about how the traditional weavers of Laos are "resources keepers" (Wallman) that provide the "fabric of health" for the community (Janzen). "Women weave their lives, hopes and aspirations into textiles" (Connors), and thus "shape the well-being of their families" (Lundberg). Indeed, the romance of "weaving as well-being" is an elegant perfume, especially for those already suffering a passion for textile art.

However, seeking a balanced and healthy family and community is ultimately a pragmatic virtue. There is nothing impractical about embracing a lifestyle and heritage that promotes "being well" and "doing well" day by day, year by year, generation by generation. And despite the twentieth-century disruptions of colonization, war, and isolation, and despite being in a rural corner of one of the world's most cash-poor nations, the people of Houaphan Province, and particularly its southern Xam Tai and Meung Kuan Districts, have survived with their communities and pride intact.

Opposite: A young weaver at her loom in Ban Tao.
Above: Malaithong's aunt greeting us in Ban Tao.

An ethic of industriousness and camaraderie secured the base essentials for pragmatic living: gaining food, shelter, clothing, and (ultimately) a sure sense of safety. Over time, however, deeper qualities are also necessary to maintain well-being. A successful community or citizenry that progresses from generation to generation requires the ability to transmit its cultural wisdom, values, and mores. It necessitates a deliberate effort—a communal calling—that seeks health and balance in all facets of the community's continuity: economic, social, physical, and spiritual.

The tradition of creating textiles has been rich and central to the way of life of the people of Xam Tai and Meung Kuan Districts for uncounted generations, and the "weaving way of life" continues to support, reflect, and transmit the knowledge of how to live a valued life.

## Weaving as Economic and Social Well-Being

Weaving in Xam Tai is, first and foremost, an occupation. As such, it provides both a service for the community—the creation of clothing, household and ceremonial textiles—and also generates a product for the textiles' creators to sell or barter. For many of the communities in the region, weaving has been and continues to be the community's sole access to cash or trade beyond excess food grown in the fields or materials collected in the forest.

Three generations of Tai Dam (Black Tai) weavers. They raise, spin, dye, and weave cotton for shirts and sinh.

It is the cash brought in by a weaver that allows a household to purchase a new metal plow, a small tractor, or a gas-powered rice thresher.

Creating textiles is primarily the task of women. Men often participate in sericulture (raising silkworms) and usually construct the floor looms and weaving tools, but the silk reelers, dyers, designers, and weavers are, with rare exception, women. Thus, the perpetuation of weaving skills gives the daughter a means to obtain life's necessities.

This role has granted local women a unique power and status—there's nothing like being a breadwinner to generate empowerment. Indeed, a woman's time spent weaving is of essential economic value, and many households have been and still are dependent on the income and trade value of that effort. In the twenty-first century, textile creators are able to generate earnings to afford school tuition (including college), modern appliances, and even real estate. Ardent weavers earn as much as government workers, and thus weaving is considered a respectable, valuable skill—with flexible hours!

In modern developing nations, often a surge of workers migrate to the city to provide an inexpensive labor pool for industry. In Laos, as well, many weavers over the recent decades have moved to the Vientiane area in search of greater participation in the cash economy. However, in a region such as Xam Tai District, where weaving is so dominant an activity, a weaver can remain in her remote village if she chooses, as long as she has a contact who can get her completed textiles to market. (This business contact is often a regional dyer, and we'll examine this economic relationship when we visit Souksakone in Chapter 27.) Such an arrangement allows the weaver to live and raise her children in the traditional setting in a traditional manner. The effect is that families are more likely to remain intact, and thus the methods of traditional cultural transmission also remain intact.

Despite fading eyes and arthritis, Me Tau Lu sat nearly every day for more than eighty years at her loom and contributed to her family's needs and the village economy. Her daughters and granddaughters live nearby, and several are active weavers. Her great-granddaughter, still too young to sit at the loom, watches everyone weave every day and absorbs the contemplative and vital efforts of her elders. At age seven or eight, she too will be invited to participate at the loom.

What practical and social skills will Me Tau Lu's great-granddaughter learn by participating in the weaving?

First, like any honed skill, the values of practice, focus, and patience will be reinforced.

Second, the values of industriousness and efficiency will likewise be reinforced.

Third, the wise and clever use of natural resources, including the building of the loom, the raising of the silk, and the creation of the natural dyes, supports the value of collaborating with the gifts that nature offers and reaffirms that working with nature (tomasat) generates greater health and well-being.

Fourth, the physical textile itself speaks to values of modesty, warmth, and protection.

Fifth, the act of weaving reinforces the value of maintaining healthy social relationships across generations. Lundberg writes: "The skill depicts and teaches core values of mutual participation, companionship and industriousness that Lao regard as essential for well-being." The fact that weaving is an activity usually done outdoors in sight of neighbors, and often in shared space, speaks to the pleasure and value of having such companionship and support. That these weavers vary from seven to ninety years of age secures a cultural foundation of shared time, experiences, stories, and mentoring.

Because the art of creating a textile so often requires a team of experts—a sericulturist, reeler, dyer, designer, weaver, and salesperson—other essential characteristics of social well-being are also reinforced. Both loyalty and honesty are vital in cooperative economic endeavors, especially in a world where written contracts (and indeed, writing at all) rarely play a role. One's word is one's bond.

We've also noticed a lot of flirting at the loom of young women. Young men will often be found after a day in the fields hovering next to a loom of a sweetheart, and young weavers often make shoulder bags or "love tokens" to give to young men they wish to impress. The giving of a handwoven cloth conveys powerful feelings in Laos, and is a symbol of commitment and affection both in casual life and formal ceremony.

Of course, not all women are weavers. Weaving requires a developed patience and desire, and participating as a "novice-in-training" demands a sharp-mind and an attentive demeanor in a girl. More than one weaver has acknowledged that the better weavers also have excellent mathe-

Young women weave as often as possible in Xam Tai.

Three daughters of Seuk share a break between chores.

matical and organizational skills. If weaving is not the youth's calling, there are many other essential roles in a community that need attention, most related to food production and animal husbandry. Often the choices for a young girl's participation in the family's and community's essential tasks, aside from school attendance, is to work at the loom or in the field (except during planting and harvest season, when everyone may be called to work in the fields). That said, Findly notes that about 90 percent of the women in Xam Tai are skilled in the basics of weaving.

One more thing: Because of the value of a weaver's time, the men in the region have a strong tradition of helping the household create the time for this effort. We often will see men in Xam Tai and Meung Kuan with children on their hips or tending to cooking and other household duties. This balance in gender relationships provides part of the foundation for cultural health. Men and women seem to hold a deep respect for their roles and contributions in the community; the well-being for all depends upon their mutual economic and familial contributions.

## Weaving as the Transmission of Culture

As mentioned before, textiles created for clothing were, at one time, cultural identifiers, with specific designs indicating specific cultural lineage and identity. However, that era has mostly passed, as has much of the knowledge about which specific features indicated what specific heritage.

While wearing specific designs as a family and clan identifier is no longer strictly adhered to, weaving does immerse the learner in a world full of cultural symbolic meaning, which creates a context for the transmission of ancestral knowledge. In essence, passing down the traditions of textile creation and symbolic design still ensures the continuity of the broader ethnic traditions, beliefs, and mores.

It is not that the textiles represent cultural identity; rather, maintaining a weaving culture—that is, the actions of the participants—literally transmits knowledge from one generation to the next as to how to live and be well.

This transmission starts by saturating the participants with social interactions between generations, as it is not only the dutiful and proud mother who teaches her daughter, but also the ever-present gray-

Siblings care for each other while parents are working.

A woman's hands are indicative of her latest dyeing effort.

ing grandmother, and perhaps the bent great-grandmother as well. Skill progression requires time and patience, offering ample time for conversation and story, telling between the generations.

Some of the shared stories will conjure up images of pregnant serpents (*naak*), mythical elephant-lions (*siho*) and fierce protective spirits (*phii-nyak*). Other tales will speak the myth-stories of how the first humans were born from deity-planted gourd seeds, and how the river dragon (*ngueak*) protects the local source of drinking water and irrigation. All these images are found in symbolic representation on both daily wear and ceremonial textiles. The history, the beliefs, the myths—they are literally woven into the material of their lives.

Of course, also shared are important tales of wartime survival, and how great-grandmother learned to swim in the river, and how mom was wooed by dad. And how to best cook a duck. And how some greens seem to glow next to certain hues of red. And on. It is important stuff—the stuff that teaches how to lead a confident and satisfying life, and how to be an active and creative member in the human endeavor to survive with purpose and integrity.

Continued on page 94

## THE BACI CEREMONY

On our first visit to Xam Neua in 2006, our guide, Kaiphet, introduced us to Phanla Pelavong, the Chairwoman of the Xam Tai Region Women's Weaving Cooperative, a government-supported affiliation of silk weavers eager to gain access to markets. She had some outstanding examples of local talent, and shared with us her knowledge of the best weaving from nearby villages.

On our second visit a few months later, we again shared time together and again purchased a selection of silk textiles. Her expertise led us to visit several local villages renowned for weaving talent: Nakham, Muang Vaen, Saleui, and Xam Tai. Her selection of textiles on this second visit was more limited. "If only you had let me know you were coming, I would have had more," she said, through Kaiphet.

In an effort to provide greater support and gain some excellent textiles in the future, we naively "placed an order" with her for some silks to be woven—we even chose two traditional styles we thought would do well in our western market. We left her with enough money to purchase the completed textiles at her fair market price.

Well, it didn't work out. With scattered and inconsistent communication systems, a kindhearted but young translator, and the fact that few westerners "order" designs—well, all this demanded that both we and Ms. Pelavong negotiate a steep cultural learning curve.

Everyone was honest; everyone had the best of intentions. But nothing seemed to get the wheels turning, and poor Kaiphet must have felt a weight of responsibility to resolve expectations that were not clearly understood, doable, or familiar to those involved. Even our third visit some months later left the issue unresolved, for Ms. Pelavong was out of town during the few days of our visit.

It was nearly two years later before we sat down again with Ms. Pelavong. She felt bad that she had not been able to follow through, but we all cheerily sat down and completed our business the old-fashioned way: cash for what was available.

To ensure the health of our relationship, and to make sure all amends were made and our friendship confirmed, Ms. Pelavong also requested that our family be her guests for a traditional Baci ceremony.

Ari, at age fifteen, wrote about the Baci Ceremony to satisfy three personal needs: as credit for tenth-grade English, to placate a dad demanding a business newsletter article, and, unbeknownst to us at the time, as an opportunity to share a unique cultural experience with you.

We had met Ms. Phanla Pelavong a couple of years earlier, and had bought quite a few silk textiles from her that had been made by the weavers she knew. On our last trip, she and her husband invited us to a special Baci ceremony and dinner in our honor.

I asked our translator, Kaiphet, what a Baci ceremony was for. He said it is a ceremony that makes sure that your *khoune*, a guardian spirit that brings you happiness, prosperity, and good luck, is united with your physical body. If the khoune is forced to leave your body, perhaps because you were scared or sick, then your body and your spirit become imbalanced. The Baci ceremony makes sure that the spirit and body are back in harmony. Kaiphet also told me that it was a pretty common ceremony, and is often performed when people have a baby, get married, or for the family after someone dies. It's also done to welcome someone special, or say goodbye, or when someone gets a big job promotion or a new home. In other words, it is kind of an excuse to celebrate or heal together if for any reason that seems an important thing to do. In this case, this Baci was to welcome us, show respect, make sure we had a good journey, wish us business success, and express friendship.

When we arrived at Ms. Pelavong's house, it was crowded with about twenty members of her extended family. A Baci is a big occasion. The Baci began with everyone sitting around a gift of candles and flowers called a *phakhouane*, which entices the good spirits to be near. The table also held bunches of yellow and white twine, called Baci strings, as well as pieces of boiled chicken, sticky rice, money, hard-boiled eggs, and other ceremonial items. Ms. Pelavong presented us each with a silk scarf we wrapped around our shoulders.

The leader of the Baci, called a *mophone*, who in this case was an older friend of Ms. Pelavong, conducted the ritual chanting. We all sat around the centerpiece cross-legged and it seemed right to bow our heads a little as she half-hummed and half-chanted what sounded to me like the same thing over and over for an awfully long time. And when the mophone put her hands together (as you do when you greet someone in Laos with a "sabaidee"), we all put our hands together too. At one point in the ceremony, everyone in my family shared a piece of chicken and some rice. They also offered an egg to both my brother and me, which we ate right away. It was already 7:30 pm, a very late dinner for us.

After eating the ritual foods, the mophone held out the yellow strings that had been braided and blessed by monks in the local temple. The mophone now stroked our hands with the strings while chanting what Kaiphet translated as "Good spirits in, bad spirits out…" over and over again. The droning, repetitive chant reminded me of the chants sung by Gregorian monks. The mophone then tied the blessed strings around our wrists and told us that we were not allowed to take the strings off until we were safely home and our journey complete. Kaiphet explained that the strings symbolized that the body and the spirit are now tied together tightly.

After the chanting finished, all of the members of Ms. Pelavong's family, including the children, tied the white strings around our wrists in a similar manner, first brushing the strings across our palm from wrist to fingertip three times, saying "out with the bad," and then three times in the other direction, saying, "in with the good."

Then everyone wished us good luck, good travels, safe return home, etc. This was the time for spontaneous good wishes and some silliness. The little kids now all got strings tied on too, and we joked about how my twelve-year-old brother should get engaged to Ms. Pelavong's twelve-year-old daughter. The little kids all ran around as if it were Christmas until dinner was finally served.

Dinner was a grand collection of dishes that were laid out in front of us on a long woven plastic mat. These dishes included bamboo rat steamed in a banana leaf, vegetable soup with slices of coagulated water buffalo blood, sticky rice, boiled chicken, and *laap*, a traditional dish served to special friends made of banana flowers, minced meat, cilantro, and lemongrass. They were all delicious with the exception of the rat, which must be an acquired taste.

After the meal, mom and dad selected some gorgeous textiles that Ms. Pelavong presented that were from local weavers. Then, finally, we walked the few blocks back to our guesthouse and quickly fell asleep.

*—Ari Hirschstein*

## AFTERWORD

The year after the Baci ceremony, Ms. Pelavong and her family moved to Vientiane to pursue other opportunities and provide the best schooling for her growing children. Also, by now our family had developed personal relationships directly with many silk artists in the small villages that Ms. Pelavong had represented, effectively bypassing her in the business relationship.

We miss her, but have little doubt that someday we will be walking along, perhaps in Xam Neua or perhaps Vientiane, and there, walking towards us, will be the bustling Ms. Pelavong. We will all smile and "Sabaidee" each other, and then, no doubt, inquire about the health of each other's children.

Left: Figure in Xam Tai's Buddhist temple. Center: A weaver's friendly smile. Right: The maker of this *kaen* plays his instrument.

### Weaving as Support for the Healers Who Seek Physical and Spiritual Well-Being

In Xam Tai, as in much of Laos, tradition holds that the physical and the spiritual aspects of our selves are not easily separated, and part of this is born from the complexity of interwoven world-paradigms.

The Lao Loum tradition, as mentioned before, is one of Theravada Buddhism; the Tai Daeng tradition is one of animism and ancestor worship. Being as these two ethnicities have cooperated and striven together for success in Xam Tai and the region, it may come as no surprise to find a hybridized—or better, harmonized—set of traditions that merge into its own particular expression.

Theravada Buddhism conceives of Buddha as a teacher—someone who points the way to a better life—rather than as a deity (as found in Mahayana Buddhism). It is the teachings of the Buddha, and not the Buddha himself, that are to be revered. The Buddhist doctrines most clearly understood and followed by non-monks are those that have the greatest impact on daily life, and thus the concepts of kharma, rebirth, and ensuring a better future through earning merit have been readily adopted by lay adherents.

Animism, however, is focused not on achieving enlightenment, but rather on helping a person cope with daily life. A foundational animist belief is that things outside of ourselves, both animate and inanimate, may harbor spiritual power, which can affect the "life-force" within oneself that defines one's well-being. An illness or misfortune would be the result of an imbalance in one's personal "life-force" due to this exterior power.

Theravada Buddhism and animism are not necessarily in conflict with each other. The tradition of striving for harmony and balance through our deliberate actions as an individual, as a family, and as a community is fundamental to both beliefs, and to the Lao mindset. In fact, in this region both Buddhists and animists have traditions that support shamanic healing and ritual offerings to the spirits of ancestors.

For the people of Xam Tai and Meung Kuan Districts, textiles, and in particular the intricate ceremonial cloths, have played a significant role for the shaman.

A stone naga adorns the stairway to a small town's Buddhist temple.

Ellie Findly's *Spirits in the Loom* details the region's blending of Buddhist and animist traditions, the practices of modern, traditional shamanism and the role of textiles in ceremony, and she speaks of how a healer can "use the motifs" in a textile to "speak to" and affect the spirits. Motifs of lanterns allude to "lighting the pathway to the spirit world"; boats transport the shaman to the spirit world; ladders and waterways allow the "good spirits in, and bad spirits out," echoing the mophone's chant in a Baci ceremony (see the next chapter). Serpents, elephant-lions, and giant spirits—these are all able to assist the shaman at her or his task.

However, Maren and I have not witnessed a shamanic ceremony in Xam Tai; these events are rare and not necessarily public or "invite-the-falang" affairs. As well, Maren and I are hesitant to dig into deep-rooted religious affiliations and beliefs; it seems inappropriate to bring the topic up beyond our desire to understand the traditions. Such personal, spiritual details not only are difficult to convey and translate, but tread on sensitive feelings that, no doubt, also overlap the politics of the community and Laos as a whole.

Like Thailand, Laos's government refers to itself as a Buddhist nation. This is not only because a significant majority of people in Laos identify as Buddhists, but also because the modern world of scientific discovery, technology, and progress aligns with Buddhism's modern worldview.

Indeed, the age of animist belief and healing is quickly fading as modern opportunities and outside interactions become more accessible and common. Nationalized schools are unifying the people through language and other curricula. Cell phones, diesel buses, cans of Pringles, jars of face-whitener, uniformed policemen, anti-bacterial soap, television soap operas, pop music on the karaoke machine, Facebook on your phone, hydroelectric projects, Nike shoes, sunburned falang tourists traipsing through your village—these things, and a hundred more, do not, in general, support or embrace the traditional animist worldview.

Further—and this can sound blunt—the adherence to an animist tradition is perceived by some people, in Laos as in every modern nation, to be "primitive" and of a time before people had access to scientific knowledge and multicultural communications. The individuals we engage with in Xam Tai, (and for that matter, the nation of Laos) would prefer to be recognized as modern people with modern aspirations, for indeed they are. And certainly, any local host who engages in business and social interactions with visiting falang would want to put their modern foot forward.

The tradition of Lao Loum and Tai Daeng motifs and design, however, does live on—both in Xam Tai and across all of Laos—and the blending of animist and Buddhist iconography that developed in this region continues to impact textile design for both the Lao and tourist markets.

This slow, multigenerational transition to a more Buddhism-inclined population generates changes. Recently we inquired about the traditional motif of what academics and local weavers have in the past referred to as an "ancestor spirit on the back of an elephant-lion." It is a motif handed down through the animist Tai Daeng tradition. "No, no," we were corrected by our Buddhist companion. "This motif is of a beautiful lady, and she rides on the elephant during a parade in Luang Prabang."

In truth, we ultimately bring to our symbolic world our own world of experience.

### Weaving as Aesthetic Expression

Finally, we'd be remiss not to acknowledge the raw artistic integrity of the textiles and the expert expression of the traditional artists who reel, dye, design, and weave silk.

In Xam Tai and Meung Kuan, we have met a collection of artists who think in colors and dream of patterns—artists whose relentless effort to find balance and stimulation motivates them to explore the boundaries of their cultural expression. Artists who live their art with all its possibilities and responsibilities.

CHAPTER FIFTEEN

# Sinh and Other Daily-Use Textiles

We want to draw a clear picture: The men and women of Xam Tai, though renowned for their amazing, millennia-old silk-raising, dyeing, and weaving skills, do not don silk finery in their daily lives. Silk clothing does not make for practical wear, and it is either time-consuming to make or expensive to purchase.

Indeed, if you were to stand in the center of Xam Tai today, with its shiny bank and modern marketplace and drive-through gas station, and look at the clothing people are wearing, you would see scant evidence that this is the hub of the world's finest silk work.

Instead, you will see two standards of formality in the daily-wear clothing of adults: one for town and business tasks (often a privilege of the wealthier), and the other for fieldwork and other grubbier tasks.

Town and business-wear for men is, for those of us who love textiles, depressingly drab and western. Shirts are factory-made blends, often a loose-fitting short-sleeve broadcloth or knit. Pants are generally factory-made synthetics or cotton blends. More formal businessmen will wear socks and closed dress shoes, although most look eager, in the humidity and heat, to get back to flip-flops after hours. The factory-made clothing is often a bit ill-fitting, loose or tight. Before factory-made clothes were readily available, men wore baggy trousers and shirts woven of indigo-dyed, local cotton. Men's clothing was, and still is, generally similar in fiber and color across ethnic lines, save for ceremonial wear.

Two young weavers in Saleui display their newly-fashioned ikat sinh. Opposite: Khom Boun, in Na Sala, spins cotton on her hand-cranked wheel.

In Xam Tai there are a few formal businessmen, perhaps a bank manager or larger business owner, who might be seen in a western-style suit and tie, but such wear is relegated to the office and the wearer's business role. After work hours, everyone is casual.

A few adult men wear shorts but most, unless working in the depth of a rice paddy, choose full-length pants, even on the hottest and most casual days. We do note that some of the young teenage women in Xam Tai will sometimes don a pair of stylish western-style shorts.

Outside of the small-business community in Xam Tai, clothing seems to play no male social role and we, as outsiders, cannot distinguish male village leaders from others by their garb. In a world where cash has been rare and communities have been isolated, such superficial assumptions regarding what people wear doesn't play a significant role. Integrity is built from one's relationships with others, and it is a lifetime of decisions, not fashion, that dictates the weight of one's words.

That said, the younger unmarried set in

From left: Young men in typical teen dress. School girls in uniform giggle and hide from the camera. Man weaving a bamboo fish trap wears long pants, even in hot weather.

Xam Tai, at least those who have access to a little disposable cash, are often eager to show a little swagger after a work day, so they slip into a pair of tight-fitting denim jeans and a sharp button-down to impress whoever might be looking. Such swagger usually cannot be afforded by the majority of district inhabitants scattered in the dozens of tiny, more isolated villages.

Much of the informal clothing worn by locals in the region is "western reject." Pickup trucks with their beds full of outdated, misspelled and other unsellable-in-the-West tee shirts and pants will visit a village several times a year for a day, dumping their unsorted load unceremoniously onto a large blue-plastic tarp where the locals can hunt for cheap, ready-wear apparel for their families. We have seen western-discarded tee shirts that say everything from "I Love Pupies," to "F##k You!" Every village and every person has access to this western-reject clothing, and it is rare to find young children dressed in anything else, assuming they're dressed at all.

Women's clothing may at first glance also seem drab, and an inattentive tourist may dismiss their everyday wear as casual and western. Above the waist, most women wear a factory-made blouse, often made of cotton or acrylic. When working around home or in the garden, a women may just as readily be seen in a loose tee shirt or a "ratty old" knit shirt. A few elders in the outlying villages may still wear their indigo-dyed handspun cotton blouses that wrap and tie across the front, but western tops are the norm. Most women between twelve and fifty wear a bra for support, and sometimes, in the thick heat of a hard-working afternoon, they strip down to this layer. Lao women are generally modest, but not prudish. (As an aside, we have been told by westerners who are fluent in Lao that there is a healthy dose of bawdy humor in local banter.)

## The Sinh

However, the ubiquitous sinh—the wrap-around tube skirt worn by nearly every Lao woman regardless of ethnicity—remains the standard in every province in Laos. Some women do choose to wear pants for less-formal occasions (most noticeably wealthier or young unmarried women), but the sinh is wrapped into Lao

From left: Woman in handspun, handwoven, indigo-dyed cotton sinh while carrying a bamboo chicken basket. One woman in western pants and another in a sinh with separate tiin sinh border. Children (right) usually dress in western clothing.

culture as tightly as it is wrapped around the waist of each Lao woman.

As an introduction, we have our own tale of sinh to tell:

Maren and I were eager to come up with a parting gift for our guide, Malaithong, whose translation skills, contact, and warmth had once again, now for the third time, elevated our appreciation of and deepened our ties with the community of Xam Tai.

A day earlier we had sat in Souksakone's home poring over dozens of incredible silks trying to narrow our selection to meet our business's budget. Malaithong had shown a special affection for a stunning blue-green sinh with columns of stylized river serpents. We had purchased it thinking of our customers, but the way Malaithong had held the sinh, and rubbed an edge of it between her fingers and thumb . . . .

We had even asked Malaithong if she had wanted to buy it, as it would be less expensive to buy it directly from Souksakone than to purchase it in a market. We would have happily chosen another.

"No" she had said quietly. "It is too much." An Assistant Director of Tourism Development (as was her title then) has a regular salary, but family priorities could not accommodate such an extravagance.

On our last day with Malaithong, we paid her for her days of service—a price set by the Tourism Office—and then Maren handed her a wrapped package.

"What is this?" asked Malaithong.

"Just a little extra 'thank you' for all your help," Maren said. "We couldn't do this without you."

Inside the wrapping, of course, was the blue-green sinh.

Malaithong's eyes went wide. "Oh, you mean this is for me?" she asked. Maren nodded.

She held the folded sinh out to see its sparkle, and then hugged it against her chest. "It is so beautiful. I don't know what to say." The usually even-keeled Malaithong looked at Maren, and then threw out the one arm that wasn't holding the textile and gave Maren a hug. Her eyes teared.

That evening, Maren and I reminisced about the gift-giving, laughing that Malaithong had sure become emotional about a well-deserved tip for her several days of service. It must have been the perfect gift, we agreed.

The following year, on our next visit to Xam Tai, it was Souksakone who brought up the previous visit, recalling how the unique color of that sinh had complimented Malaithong so well. Souksakone casually commented, "I wish someone would give me a sinh."

"But Souksakone," Maren said, with Malaithong translating. "Malaithong doesn't weave. Surely you could make one for yourself." We all laughed, and Maren and I, I'm embarrassed to admit, gave it little thought beyond a moment of self-congratulations that the gift had been so well-received.

The epiphany came to us some months later thanks to Viengkham Nanthavong-douansy's *Sinh and Lao Women*. She concludes her book: "Apart from the use of sinh in traditional customs, Lao people see this garment as a communicator of love. The young give sinh to their elders to show love and respect, friends give sinh to friends to show true companionship, and a man gives a sinh to his wife or his lover to show his heart."

Several months later, Maren found herself in Phout's company, this time at Phout's daughter's home in Vientiane. Maren had been invited to join the family at an annual festival at one of Vientiane's prominent wats (temples).

At the festival, Maren and Phout's family visited a booth selling indigo-dyed handspun cotton sinh. They were simple, inexpensive daily-wear skirts but they had a particularly well-crafted ikat-style weave and a soft, luscious drape. Through her son-in-law, Phout asked if Maren would

Above, weaver in Saleui displays her naturally-dyed silk fabric still on the loom.
Right: Souksakone dresses in an elegant silk sinh for a formal occasion.

buy her one of the sinh. Maren recalled the above quote and said "Of course," and the two of them spent ten minutes selecting the pattern that best suited Phout.

Phout held the chosen sinh up to her chest and, looking Maren directly in the eyes, said a few gracious words that didn't need translating. The two spent the next two hours wandering the rest of the market holding hands.

Maren and Phout do embrace a particularly personal and trusted bond—a deep loyalty that values their affection. They have, to use Nanthavongdouansy's words, a "true companionship."

A wedding party shows a variety of traditional sinh. The most complex sinh are often worn at weddings.

## A Spark

Traditionally, a woman's sinh signified a woman's unique cultural identity. Before the influx of western culture in the 1950s and 1960s, a sinh's design would identify a woman as to her ethnicity, marital status, wealth, age, and family lineage. The representational identity of a woman was literally woven by pattern and color into her sinh. But over the last generations, as ethnic groups have blended and a multicultural national identity has been nourished, the style elements of the sinh have become less an identifier, and far more a prideful expression of "Lao-ness."

The handwoven sinh almost went out of fashion. During the years of the American War, factory-made cloth from Japan and Hong Kong flooded the Lao market; it's hard to deny the convenience of cheap synthetics. By war's end, the urban markets for silk shrank even further as foreigners (and the remnants of wealth) left and the royal court was dismantled.

In 1975, however, when Laos closed its trade borders with the rest of the world, women had to return to their traditional weaving, not only as a source of cloth, but also as a means for barter, and, with economic liberalization arriving in 1986, cash.

In fact, at this time of isolation and internal rebuilding, the Pathet Lao government transformed the Lao Women's Union from a support group of mothers of revolutionary soldiers into an organization that initiated and implemented women's projects, including those based on textile production. Van Esterik writes that policies were implemented that strongly encouraged women to wear Lao-woven sinh, and a national pride was invigorated that upheld the sinh as emblematic of the unique beauty and talent of Lao culture. Sericulture was again promoted, and experts from south Asia were even imported in some areas (especially around Vientiane where resettlement and post-War growth was centered) to re-teach weaving skills to the many communities that had, in the chaos of the previous generations, become separated from their artistic and cultural roots. In short, both government policies and economic necessity elevated the sinh to be an important modern cultural icon.

Bottom line: If you're a woman, wearing a sinh is the Lao thing to do, regardless of ethnicity. It's comfortable, friendly, and establishes a sense of community. After all, sharing is a form of joining, and the sinh creates common ground for a relationship even when ancestors, paradigms and languages vary. Even if you're falang!

In most weaving traditions in the region, cotton has been the primary fiber for clothing. Most ethnic groups, however, no longer practice their clothing-making traditions, the art having been lost or rendered obsolete. These people, like most everyone in the world, rely on the marketplace for everyday wear and they seek modestly-priced sinh woven from cotton or acrylic (many with a sprinkling of supplemental silk design). To meet the broad market's demand—after all, there are nearly four million Lao women—there are many weaving centers located especially around Vientiane and, to a lesser degree, Luang Prabang; these population and industrial centers have become an economic magnet for some rural weavers who want to tie into the twenty-first century economy.

In Xam Tai District, while silk may be more readily available than in most other rural areas, two criteria limit its regular use as a primary fiber. First, silk's value is determined by a hungry international market, which makes it expensive for the average person in Laos to purchase. Burgeoning demand in neighboring China and Vietnam, as well as markets in Europe, mostly fuel today's market. Second, most people's lives are centered on farming and other physical labor, and silk just doesn't do well in the oils, dirt, and rugged wear expected of laboring adults.

A silk sinh with a 100-percent silk warp, weft, and supplemental pattern threads would be deemed most fancy; one might see such finery at weddings or among the wealthier at important events, especially in the urban setting. The price for an exquisite handwoven silk sinh in the market in Vientiane may, if the design is complex, reach many hundreds of dollars (and is the result of several months of loom work). More common would be a poly-cotton or all-acrylic warp and weft with a touch of silk supplemental patterning; for a bit more glamor, one might choose to weave a poly-cotton warp with a silk weft, lending a beautiful shimmer but still keeping costs more modest.

The traditional sinh is comprised of three parts: the waistband (*hua sinh*), the tube skirt itself (*phaa sinh*), and the hem (*tiin sinh*).

The hua sin is usually a cotton strip twelve to twenty inches wide (30-50 cm) that attaches to the tube skirt with a tacking stitch. It not only protects the tube skirt, but also carries symbolic weight, for this panel touches the belly's skin and protects the womb. In fact, old sinh are very difficult to find with their original waistbands attached, for women will remove that section when it leaves their hands, believing that such an intimate piece of apparel, in the wrong hands, may be used against them as "black magic."

The skirt body, or phaa sinh, is traditionally of dark indigo-dyed handspun cotton; it is warm, thick, and strong, and most, from a distance, appear quite plain. Subtle stripes of red, green, or yellow—often indicators of ethnicity—may be created in the warp. Today, cotton has broadly given way to synthetic fibers, and more prominent design motifs—ones that might traditionally have been found only in ceremonial textiles—are now common in daily-wear sinh.

The hem, or tiin sinh, is traditionally woven as a separate narrow panel three to ten inches wide (8—25 cm) that is then stitched onto the bottom of the sinh. It assures that the skirt's main body is not damaged, and, from a designer's standpoint, adds an attractive horizontal stripe at the base of the vertical sinh. While traditional tiin sinh are modestly, if at all, decorated, the recent generation has chosen to celebrate the hem's design with elaborate traditional motifs: dancing dragons, parading elephants, entwining serpents, and more. Tiin sinh are also woven on a standard floor loom, albeit with a narrow warp. Warp and weft may be cotton, silk, or synthetic (or a combination), with the hand-picked supplemental design element often of silk.

A Lao woman and baby are wrapped in *phaa tuum*, with the *phii nyak*, or giant spirit pattern, woven in for protection.

The traditional three-part sinh, however, is today becoming a relic of the past, and the market for Lao sinh is now filled with "single-warp" sinh, where the skirt's full length is woven on a single warp and the tiin sinh design element is hand-picked onto the base of the skirt after each pass of the weft's shuttle. We'll revisit this significant change when we discuss the marketplace in Chapter 38.

Still, while the design elements of the sinh may be evolving, the pride of the sinh seems undiminished. Today, throughout Laos, wearing the handwoven sinh functions as a unifier—a source of national pride and a symbol of community. It is one way for so many different women from so many different ethnic traditions—women who have fought so hard and endured so much—to bond together, tightly woven.

## Other Household Textiles

Before a young woman in Xam Tai is married, tradition holds that she must

weave a selection of household textiles as part of her dowry. Today, factory-made household textiles can also be readily bought in the market, but given the weaving talent of the community, many of these items are still made in the home.

Typically, a traditional newlywed's home would require pillows, bedding, a mosquito net border, door curtains, and blankets.

Few homes offer chairs or couches; instead, locals weave cotton-covered cushions (*phaa nang*) about fourteen inches square (35 cm) and three inches thick (8 cm). Because of their constant use, locals use a durable poly-cotton warp and weft for the phaa nang, with a simple discontinuous supplemental silk or cotton motif woven on the top. Red is the preferred color although the bottom panel is often black. The pillows may be stuffed with kapok, cotton, or cast-off fabric, and those of us who are honored guests (and have bigger bottoms) are offered two or more to sit upon. Many homes also have triangular "leaning pillows" (*morn tao*) for your back if a deeper recline is needed. After a day of work in the fields (or at the loom), I can imagine that leaning back to take the pressure off must be welcomed respite.

Traditional mattresses are made much the same way, except that top and bottom are indigo-dyed black cotton (or chemical-dyed poly-cotton) and there is no need for a design element; the narrow sides, as with the pillows, are red. White cotton sheeting then usually covers the mattress. From a western perspective, these mattresses are pretty thin and hard; from this middle-aged guy's perspective, factory-made mattresses are a welcome addition.

Pillows are used only for casual reclining. If one is doing seated work, a short wicker stool is almost always preferred.

A mosquito-net border (*poei*) is a twenty-foot-long (7 m), twelve-inch-wide (30 cm) band of fabric with elaborate supplemental decoration that encircles the bed

An elder woman iin Xam Tail wraps herself in a mosquito-net border she wove for her trousseau as a teenager.

at standing-head level; it is attached to the tops of posts (or the wall) above each of the bed's four corners. Draped from this woven band, plain black cotton yardage hangs to the floor; black cotton also covers the "roof" of the bed. This protection offers two benefits: it protects the bed's occupants from nighttime mosquitos, and it creates a private setting for a couple in an otherwise communal room.

The length of the mosquito-net border offers modern collectors an elaborate shape to play with, and the bands of design often offer appropriate motifs of stars, moons, and mythical creatures born of dreams. Some borders offer a repetitive design, with each stripe of supplemental work being essentially identical. The finest examples of poei, however, offer unique designs for each of the dozens of stripes that make up the textile, thus showing off the weaver's investment of time and talent.

These borders are more a "were" than an "are." Pre-shaped factory-produced mosquito nets are inexpensive and let more breeze through; many homes now have metal bug screens hinged on their window frames and avoid nets altogether. The only mosquito net borders we commonly encounter now are ones that elders wove in their youth, and which have been sitting in a closet or clothing basket for years (usually with their plain black cotton sides cut off and repurposed).

In a traditional home, the living area is separated from the sleeping area with a wooden or woven bamboo wall, and a narrow door curtain (*phaa kang*) is woven to hang as a screen in the doorway between the two rooms. These curtains are almost all woven from poly-cotton, as both cotton and silk are too fragile for the constant use these textiles endure. Phaa kang usually display decorative discontinuous weft designs woven on a red or black background, and they are hung unhemmed and without backing. Those that need to be fitted to a doorway are bordered with plain white, red, or black material, or sometimes with flowery Chinese-made and printed acrylic fabric. The motifs are usually large and obvious, and tend towards mythical creatures or forest or farm animals.

Because nighttime winter temperatures can drop to near freezing, every home also needs blankets for warmth. Today, most households prefer commercially-made blankets; indeed, the thick Chinese-made poly-cotton quilts are a welcome weight when snuggling into bed on a cool evening.

I understand why these thick acrylics were so readily adopted: traditional sleeping blankets (*phaa hom*) are thin and undersized—especially for those of us who are more "western-proportioned." While designs varied, most handwoven phaa hom have a decorated center panel about three feet by five feet (1 m x 1.7 m) encircled by a six- to ten-inch (15–25 cm) plain cotton border which is tidily folded and sewn at each corner; many phaa hom are additionally backed with a panel of handspun cotton sheeting. The center panels may be of one full-width weft, or may be of two narrower half-width panels that are sewn together with a center seam. Designs most often involve narrow stripes and/or interlocking geometric motifs. Sleeping blankets may be of either cotton or silk, or have a cotton warp and silk weft; the supplemental yarns may also be of either cotton or silk. The mix of cotton and silk yields a medium weight blanket that is quite warm.

Xam Tai and Meung Kuan District's weavers also create shoulder-wrap blankets (*phaa tuum*), which are used as shawls during the day, both for warmth and as a wrap to hold and carry a child. Phaa tuum are woven as one long narrow textile, almost always in white cotton with indigo-dyed supplements that generate a repetitive black-and-white geometric pattern of a chosen motif. The weaver then creates a narrow design using discontinuous supplemental weft near each of the ends of the textile; the final few inches of the length is left in plain weave with no design at all. The plain-weave ends are then zone dyed using natural lac dye; that is, the red dye is painted onto the warp threads while the textile is still on the loom; the weaver then finishes the ends with a red silk weft. This entire six-foot-long (2 m) textile is then taken off the loom, cut in half, and the two sections sewn side by side to form a long center seam. The top edge is hemmed, with the discontinuous supplemental and plain-weave zone-dyed bands aligning at the blanket's bottom edge.

While one would be hard-pressed to find weavers of phaa hom blankets in the twenty-first century, we still find many people weaving and using the traditional-style phaa tuum. Why this one particular unique and distinctive textile—the only style where we see zone dyeing—remains popular in village use is, perhaps, because its iconic design has come to represent the close bond between mother and child. (Neither of us has ever seen a man using one.) Not inappropriately, many of the phaa tuum prominently display the one-eyed *phii-nyak* motif—a fierce ancestral spirit that protects the young.

Warmth, comfort, protection—some things, perhaps, just shouldn't change.

CHAPTER SIXTEEN

# Ta of Meung Kuan

It's 2015, and Meung Kuan is a town in mid-transformation. The old village, at the bottom of the slope, still displays its few dozen stilted homes. Above this sleepy hamlet, however, engineers and bulldozers have platted a perfectly square crosshatch of cement streets, each with covered drainage and sidewalks. A dozen large construction projects on the hillside mark that Meung Kuan is being converted into an important new district headquarters, complete with a hospital, government offices, and modern schools for the district's secondary students (who previously had to live and attend in Xam Tai). It is, as such, an outpost of modern opportunity, and proof that change comes to all corners.

Maren and I, having left our duffel in the room of Meung Kuan's new (and only) hotel, emerge in the hot mid-morning sun and open our umbrellas—"traveler's shade." Malaithong, our guide, had disappeared earlier with a friend, and we knew she wanted to prepare a meal to share with the new district's governor's wife. ("Yes," Malaithong confirmed. "She is a cousin of mine…"). What better than a walk through town? Perhaps we'd find a woman sitting at the loom, or an elder weaving a basket.

Walking quietly among the homes, it takes only a minute to find two looms sitting in the shade. On one of the looms, the exposed portion of the woven silk reveals an unusual motif in bold stripes of yellow and orange. The depth of the colors and their subtle earth tones suggest it is naturally dyed (which we confirmed later). The motif in the tapestry-weave center portion of her phaa biang is of a recurring phii-nyak, a powerful, even vicious, spirit that protects children and is more often displayed on children's blankets.

But this one displays a slightly edgier geometry. A unique balance.

"Sabaidee," Maren intones loudly as she steps close to the textile still attached to the loom. The weave is crisp and the center panel of tapestry weave appears nearly seamless; the motif's edges are sharp and consistent.

"Oh…" a woman pokes her head out of the doorway up above us, on the landing of the stilted home. She disappears a moment and then comes through the door curtain, tightening her sinh, and smiles. "Sabaidee-ee."

"Are you the weaver?" Maren asks in Lao. Maren acts the words as she speaks, pointing to the woman, then the loom, and then mimicking how the locals use the loom's comb as the beater.

The woman shakes her head and laughs. "*Bo*," she chortles, and she rattles off a fast sentence. Maren hears the word for daughter, *luk sau*, in the sentence and steers a short conversation with her few Lao words, learning that her daughter is fifteen years old.

Maren returns to the fine piece on the loom and openly admires it, murmuring the word for beautiful, *ngam*, several times loudly enough for the mother to hear.

After a few more pleasantries, including our gaining the Lao word for "orange," (*maak-giang*, the same as the fruit), Maren asks (and acts out) if there is anyone, at her home or anywhere close by, with more textiles like this one.

The woman quickly acknowledges that she has some, if we could

Ta is wearing a sinh of her own design and weaving.

form: a white blouse and dark sinh with a simple white tiin sinh at the hem. We praise her meticulous work and she smiles shyly. Her mother stands off to one side with a suppressed smile and remains silent, letting Ta soak up the attention.

Ta confirms before we could ask that she had not only woven the textile using discontinuous supplemental weft and tapestry-style weaving, but also had designed the unique symmetry of the textile's central phii-nyak motif. All of her previous pieces have used the template patterns of others; this is one of her first full silk creations that uses her personal design.

We tell her we feel honored to represent her work, and we encourage her to continue—surely she has the qualities of a master weaver if she continues to hone her craft.

The following year, 2016, we return to visit Ta and her mother. We want to share the photo we had taken of her the previous year (another copy was given to the textile's purchaser in the U.S.). Of course, we also want to know if she has any more textiles for sale, which she does.

We also want permission, from her and her mother, to take some new photos.

Ta laughs quietly, holding her hands in front of her mouth. "Yes," she whispers shyly. Ta looks around quickly at the small crowd of neighbors and friends who have gathered. She says something that causes the group to laugh, and then dashes into her home.

Bobbins of silk wait their turn at the shuttle.

"She says she has to change clothes," says Malaithong. "She says she has a favorite sinh that she weaves, and she wants to wear that for the photo." Ta emerges after five minutes—a long time if you're a waiting crowd—wearing a fresh blouse and tightening her own handwoven sinh on her waist. Her face is touched with makeup.

"Sit here on the loom," we request through Malaithong. She nervously perches on the bench, initially looking at the ground in front of her, she then she slowly lifts her eyes to catch glances at her friends and her family, and us falang. She giggles and again tries to hide her mouth behind her hands.

"Maren wants to ask you a few questions, about your weaving?" Malaithong translates.

Ta giggles again. "*Bo pengyan*," she says quietly. No problem. Malaithong pulls her stool closer to Ta and leans in to hear her soft answers.

Ta was not born in Meung Kuan, but like many in town, she is the member of a village that had recently relocated to this new district's headquarters. She first started weaving at age five with her mother's help, creating simple tiin sinh. She brags with a shy laugh that she sold that very first piece in the local market!

Her mother, beaming a big smile, breaks in: "Everyone around here knows Ta is an excellent weaver!"

Yes, Ta acknowledges. She does have a gift with weaving, and she admits to "thinking all the time about colors and patterns." Though she usually works with a set pattern template, she has recently been doing some of her own unique design work, as with the phii-nyak we had bought the previous year.

"The tapestry weave?" Ta rolls her eyes. She is smiling now, and sitting upright with her hands casually reaching out to her loom. "The threads are so close together, and it takes so long…."

She prefers to weave sinh. They are quick to make, each taking only about ten days (forty hours), and they sell quickly. A complex phaa biang, like the one we had purchased, can take a couple months. Ta also confesses she likes to weave most what sells in the market. Nothing confirms success like sales.

She weaves just about every day after school, perhaps for three or four hours. The trade-off is that she rarely has to help in her family's rice fields and garden, even in the harvest season. They have enough labor for those tasks. Ta's time is more valuable as a skilled weaver.

Her dream for the future, like most young women her age, is to "work in an office." Which makes sense. In a world not far removed from subsistence farming and relentless physical labor, having confidence in a "desk-job paycheck" would generate feelings of comfort and security.

But, Ta confesses (and here she glances at her mother), "Even with an office job, I will probably still weave, at least after work."

CHAPTER SEVENTEEN

# Ceremonial Textiles

The traditional shaman healers of the region, who could (and still can) be either women or men, needed unusual clothing that sets them apart from laypeople. Cheesman writes: "When shamans wore textiles in trance they became spirits and dressed so the ancestors would recognize and accept them. The dead also had to be dressed for the same reasons. Their dress incorporated symbols and motifs that protected and assisted them on their journeys to the other world."

For millennia—back to the dawn of the culture's cohesion—the creation and use of textiles has been central to the Lao-Tai expression of maintaining health and balance in one's personal and community life. Indeed, the unique blend of traditions that has nurtured Xam Tai's well-being has embraced textile art in virtually every ceremony that acknowledges the human experience: birth, marriage, death, protection from the spirits, and physical, mental, and spiritual healings.

Opposite: A traditional shaman cloth with saang hong, a naak boat with khon buhaan, and small animal designs.

To appeal to a western romantic audience, we would love to say that the creators of the textiles "weave their souls into every cloth," and that the power of a shaman's cloth in a healing ceremony is, in essence, harnessing some vital power imbued into the textile thanks to the "life-force" of the textile's creator.

But that's not true.

Yes, the designs and the motifs that are woven carry meaning, and ritual use of textiles during ceremony does bring about, to borrow Findly's words, "significant transformation, personally or communally, in Lao-Tai lives."

And yes, we have been told that tradition holds that the character motifs of a textile, such as the river serpent or hong bird, are deliberately "hidden" in geometric complexity so that a healer may enter a room where there are ill-serving spirits and, essentially, "sneak in" the hidden good spirits in the cloth and affect a healing.

Such raw imagery is captivating!

We wondered, when we were first introduced to ceremonial textiles, if hanging a ritual shaman's shawl on a wall for decoration might be inappropriate. Might it insult someone who holds a firm conviction in the power of the spirits? Or what if we took a pair of shears to a healing cloth for a personal textile project—would that be disrespectful? In essence, does the cloth itself hold power or sacredness?

When we asked this of our Xam Tai friends, they laughed. "How could that be?" The textile is, after all, only cloth, an assemblage of fibers. It carries no meaning or power unless a trained shaman ascribes such meaning and power to it. A shaman may use a cloth ritualistically to invoke the spirits, but the cloth is merely a tool.

At least so we've been told by the few we've asked. But we have not asked a shaman, nor sought the counsel of those who still fully embrace the traditional animist interpretation of the spiritual and corporeal worlds.

The era of shamanic healing and using ceremonial cloths for their traditional purpose is nearly over. Modern medicine, education, and communications have supplanted much of the need for traditional healings and spiritual cleansing. That said, there are still active shamans today, and local textiles are still used as tools by them to effect healings and facilitate other ceremonies. They are especially evident in the complex funeral rites that assure the spirit of

the person who has died successfully crosses to the next realm.

However, while shamanism may be diminishing, the art and tradition of weaving textiles associated with shamanism has not diminished. While certain styles of shamanic textiles, such as the headdress, may no longer be regularly woven, the beauty and symbolic nature of the textiles has captured a worldwide audience, and thus the weavers of Xam Tai still weave healing and other shaman-style textiles—not necessarily for a shaman's use (although they may be used as such), but as a source of income, an expression of art, and as a foundation for cultural continuity.

This modern incentive for weaving shamanic textiles—to sell them as art and décor to tourists and textile enthusiasts—has had an impact on design. The most noticeable change is the color palette. Traditional ceremonial textiles almost always had a warp and weft in red (or rarely, black); the primary supplemental weft color was usually white. However, as contemporary weavers have discovered, this new audience desires a diverse array of colors.

Our friends in Xam Tai have a name for such colors—sii falang ("color for foreigners"). Now these age-old-style traditional cloths are being woven with reimagined ground colors: turquoise, tan, sea-foam green, midnight blue. From an artistic standpoint, this has added a new creative element, and many artists are exploiting this freedom with color-play to birth a new generation of artistic expression. On the other hand, it is one more step away from tradition.

A man-woman healing cloth, naturally dyed and designed by Phout.

## Healing Cloths (Phaa sabai)

In Lao, phaa means cloth, and sabai means "well-being," or "health" (as in the greeting: sabai-dee). Hence, phaa sabai textiles are shawls that can be worn by either shamans or laypeople during a healing ceremony. Such ceremonies may seek to heal an individual's wound, disease, or defect (including, we've been told, getting bad grades in school); other ceremonies may seek to balance the spirits of the community, or the relationship between two families, or even to help a field be more productive. Wherever there is "bad luck" or "bad feelings," there is a need to rebalance the spirits to create sabai. These cloths provide, to use Cheesman's word, a "pathway" to get the bad spirits out, and the good spirits back in.

Traditionally, phaa sabai were woven using lac-dyed silk for both the warp and weft, and then the ends of the cloth were elaborately decorated with continuous and discontinuous supplemental silk threads in the weft. A center panel, perhaps a third the cloth's length, was left unadorned. Cloths are usually 16 to18 inches wide (40-45 cm), and vary in length from 48 to 90 inches (120-230 cm), and often have short fringes on the end made from separate yarns. Recently, many weavers in Xam Tai have included inverted silkworm cocoons at the base of the fringe, a revival of an old tradition; the result resembles a row of delicate white flowers with multi-colored silk fringe as stamens.

On phaa sabai, the symbolic decoration on each of the end panels is often identical, and the motifs can vary from a tangled "box of river serpents" to determined "two-headed elephant-birds." This iconography has been described by academics as a symbolic story of the fierce motif's chasing the spirits from one end of the textile to the other, and then being forced out of the human world on a stylized set of bands—a "ladder"—at the textile's end. Thematically, motifs may be either animist- or Buddhist-related, but the truth is, as alluded to earlier, trying to separate the two beliefs in Xam Tai is like seeking to understand a textile by looking separately at its warp and weft.

A recently-introduced variation on the phaa sabai, as seen in Ta's creation in the previous chapter, turns the plain center panel into an artful display of tapestry-weaving skill, proving the artistry is evolving and seeks new expression.

One particularly striking style in Xam Neua and other villages in Houaphan Province is the "man-woman" healing cloth. These cloths have identical complex designs on both end panels, but one of the panels, the "woman's side," has bright, varied coloration, while the opposite panel, the "man's side," is completed in two muted colors. The opposing panels, upon first glance, look unrelated; upon careful inspection, however, one realizes that the panels are, in their patterning, one and the same. The women weavers laugh and nod when we acknowledge the "complexity and beauty" of the woman's half and the "simplicity and monochrome" of the male half.

The "man-woman" dichotomy in a healing cloth is representative of the inherent need in all of us to seek balance in our lives. A healthy person, just as in healthy relationships and communities, requires both empathy and endurance, nurturance and discipline, push and pull.

Phout, whom you will meet shortly, admitted in 2015 that these "man-woman" cloths that she had been creating were having a tough time finding a market, and thus she stopped having the weavers who work with her make them. "But they are stunning!" Maren blurted out. Phout nodded her head, but we understood: a person's time and materials have to provide. Pragmatism maintains that one's efforts must turn the economic wheels of running a household. Thus, for the first time since trying to order with Ms. Pelavong many years ago, we committed to ordering several "man-woman" cloths of Phout's design, which we picked up a few months later. No regrets: they are knockout beautiful, and they sold quickly.

We felt odd making such a deliberate attempt to maintain a traditional textile style. Our ethic had been to not interfere with the creative decisions of the weavers. But the truth is that our business, of course, is the market. And the market—all of it—does very much drive the momentum of the artistry.

## Shaman's Shawls (Phaa phi mon)

The apex of complexity and opulence in Xam Tai's repertoire of silks is the shaman's shawl (phaa phi mon). Traditionally, these were worn only by shamans performing a healing, and never by laypeople (unlike the phaa sabai). As woven today, they can be described as phaa sabai without the plain-weave center panel, and with the complex geometric motifs woven throughout the full length of the shawl.

Traditionally, these clothes had an indigo-dyed cotton warp and weft with silk discontinuous supplemental weft design elements woven primarily with white thread. Sizes varied from small squares to long shawls, and there was no set format for the motifs or structure. Cheesman writes: "An intense concentration of shamanic motifs and complex weaving techniques were used to create the illusion of three-dimensional images. Mythological creatures loomed out of the textiles or disappeared into the confusion of texture and colour…." Spots of intense color, representing important life events, often speckled the white-on-black design, serving to further disguise the essential healing motif underneath.

The phaa phi mon woven in Xam Tai today are not of this style, however. The ground may be of any color, and the intricate design usually incorporates a broader and more dynamic array of colors. We've noticed that some of the colorways chosen by modern weavers seem to hide the motifs in complexity; other weavers choose to use color to better manifest the symbols so the user can better see the motifs. These would be modern artistic variations, and, in some respects, this broadening, market-driven freedom to manipulate design has opened up new potential for self-expression.

Xam Tai's weavers also create "double-wide" phaa phi mon, full thirty-six-inch wide (.9 m) shawls blanketed from end to end with complex intertwining motifs. Souk, Phout and Lun, three of Xam Tai's textile leaders, describe them as "ceremonial wedding blankets." These are the most opulent, luxurious and intricate natural silk art textiles made, perhaps in the world. Their described purpose is to protect the newlyweds in their new home, and to ensure that the couple and the "children they create under the blanket" have good health, good luck, and good lives. These cloths may have a band of plain cotton stitched onto the perimeter to ensure it's wide enough to be a blanket.

We ourselves have acquired some older wide silk textiles (late nineteenth/early twentieth century) referred to as phaa phi mon, but they were described as kneeling clothes for shamans, and not as protective wedding blankets. To further confuse, one of our guiding academic texts on Lao-Tai textiles says that these wedding cloths were "invented" in 1980 (before the modern tourist market); another academic text on this region's textiles doesn't refer to them at all. Perhaps the truth just depends on whom one asks and where one is. Regardless, these broad, complex cloths have been woven and used for generations.

If one were to climb into the textile trunks of the oldest elders, other designs would emerge that are no longer being created. One older design of phaa phi mon has a single colorful Chinese-style dragon that spans end to end on a white warp and weft. This motif-character appears not to want to remain hidden at all from the spirits, but yearns to take them on straightaway. The traditions behind these older textiles quickly get murky, and answers regarding the creators' ethnic group or subgroup, the generation of creation, or the intentions and understandings of its original users have been lost (or perhaps, don't wish to be shared).

Not that these old cloths, at least aesthetically, have lost their magic and appeal to the enthusiast.

Today, phaa sabai and phaa phi mon textiles are woven to be worn as elegant shawls or displayed as wall art, and only rarely might a new textile be used by a shaman in ritual. They are woven almost always of 100 percent naturally-dyed silk, as the more refined international audience prefers. This developing market is granting more flexibility to design, and giving today's textile artists more freedom to work with the iconography and other design elements.

## Temple or Shoulder Cloths (Phaa phai)

Ceremonial silk design in traditional Xam Tai textiles does still have one style that is regularly worn by locals: the phaa phai. These are narrow (six to eight inch, 15-20 cm) strips of design and color we see worn by men and women at a Baci ceremony or in the local Buddhist temple. Women also wear these shoulder cloths at formal events such as weddings.

And perhaps for more formal photos that may appear in a book….

Phaa phai have the same design elements of the other ceremonial cloths, and may have a plainweave center panel, as healing cloths have, or may be of one complex geometric design from end to end, as shaman's cloths have. Also, like the other ceremonial textiles, traditionally phaa phai have a red or indigo warp and weft, but today the ground colors can be any hue.

They are often referred to as "women's shoulder cloths to wear to the temple," and academics align this style strongly with Buddhist tradition and wear. This may explain its broader appeal, and its broad usage across all lines of ethnicity in Laos. Its narrow design perhaps also aligns better with modern fashion and household budgets.

Regardless, the phaa phai is supported by a popular, nation-wide market, which in turn more assuredly supports that the complex motif patterns evident in ceremonial cloths will continue to be woven, and that the generational transmission of the skills and stories inherent in the creation of these cloths will remain seamless.

The phaa phai-width textile also has a traditional role in men's garments. Shamans during ceremonies may wear a narrow cloth as a head scarf or dancing shawl (phaa haang), and Buddhist monks still often wear a belt (phaa haat aeo) that looks similar: a six-inch-wide (15 cm) silk with panels of continuous or discontinuous supplemental weft designs on each end and a long center panel of plain weave.

## Other Ritual Textiles (Altar, Wedding, Funeral)

The shamans of the region have a wide variety of unusual traditional textiles beyond healing cloths associated with their ceremonial tasks. We have read that many wear elaborate costumes from head to foot during ceremony, and often a variety of textiles will be available at a healing so that a shaman may change clothes as she or he moves in and out of trance. Unique head-dresses and hats, blouses, belts, sinh (often worn by men as well), and scarves with and without rattles may be in the healer's "toolbox."

Ceremonial textiles also surround the dead. There are twenty-foot (6 m) funeral banners to be erected on tall poles outside of a mourner's home, and coffin screens to separate the deceased's belongings in a home before burial. Coffins themselves demand complex and elaborate covers. The body itself is dressed in layers of fine clothing for use in the next life, and mourners have specific clothing to wear as well, often involving white cotton.

As the age of the shaman-healer di-

Two shoulder cloths that would be worn to temple or at a Baci ceremony. Left is a moon pattern, and right is Chinese keys.

minishes, and as these previously isolated ethnic groups embrace the modernism of the twenty-first century, such rituals, and weaving the textiles for the express purpose of ceremony, likewise diminishes.

The acknowledged leaders of the textile artists in Xam Tai—those at the forefront of the art and the business—express an obligation to follow both tradition and the market. They understand that the culture and community, to maintain its well-being, must adhere to certain traditions. On the other hand, future success demands adjusting to the inevitability of modernity and the pragmatism of earning a living in today's world.

Left: Eighty- to ninety-year-old shaman cloth from Bounkeo's home village. This has been used in decades of shaman ceremonies. It is natural-dyed silk with a handspun cotton border. Above: Phouey modeling her husband's Tai Daeng grandmother, Me Tau Hom's, shaman skirt and shaman headscarf end. Opposite: A closer look at the shaman skirt and headscarf.

CHAPTER EIGHTEEN

# Phout of Xam Tai

The heat and humidity of the day was starting to lift, and the long shadow of the far hill finally reached the front of Souksakone's home where several of us sat immersed in our quiet projects. Maren was making notes in her buying journal; Souksakone, her daughter, and Malaithong were in the kitchen. Souksakone's husband, Hamman, sat at the table with two other men and talked quietly in Lao—perhaps about the day's work, perhaps about the weather.

Everyone looked up at the approaching "pop-pop-pop" of a motorcycle and then the long squeal of dusty brakes. Even before the engine was cut, we heard a high "Sabai-DEEEEE" and then a gushing of words—in Lao—followed by a cheerful laugh. There was a rustling of plastic bags as the words continued, first muted and low, then loud again. As Phout came in through the open door, she continued with another run of words, the final few exploding into a series of extended vowels that turned to quick laughs.

Phout is a larger-framed Lao Loum woman; she stands several inches taller and one slight shift wider than the average woman in Xam Tai, and this, perhaps, has helped Maren and her connect with a sister-like bond over our years of visits. Today she wore a fitted western-tailored business jacket made from gold and red-toned silk with incredibly precise discontinuous supplemental wefts over a factory-made cotton blouse, and black-knit stretch yoga pants.

With her entrance, everyone's eyes bounced up; all faces wore smiles. Phout swung the several plastic bags that were wrapped around her wrists onto the table, held up her right hand, and issued what sounded like a quick declarative sentence followed by her own laughter. With all eyes on her, Phout reached her hands out in front of herself as if clenching motorcycle handles and uttered a few casual-toned sentences. As she continued talking, however, her tone rose, her eyes grew wider, and then her hands and the handlebars started to wobble back and forth—she's losing control of the bike! Phout interrupted her story with a full, round guffaw; laughter bubbled from everyone in the room.

Still holding onto the handlebars, Phout regained her voice and another flurry of words followed. Phout's hands wobbled wildly one last time and finally jumped into the air. Her voice followed

Below: Our friend Linda is hitching a ride on the back of Phout's motorcycle. Opposite: Phout at her loom.

her words, her final syllables extending skyward in a single, long high-flying vowel—"oooooooo-eeeeeee"—followed by another burst of words that collapsed in Phout's own laughter.

Everyone fell to gales of laughter, Maren and I included.

Phout regained her breath and then suddenly locked eyes with Maren, whom she had not seen in nearly a year. She walked up to Maren and took hold of both of her hands. Phout smiled, confirmed Malaithong was listening, and spoke a couple of hushed sentences. Malaithong translated: "Phout says she is very glad to get here safely, and she is so grateful to see you." Phout looked directly into Maren's eyes as Malaithong continued translating. "She says she thinks of you often and has wished for this day to arrive for a long time." Phout shook Maren's hands up and down slightly in rhythm with Malaithong's patient words. "And Phout says she has many beautiful textiles to show you, too, but most of all she hopes you will have time to share with her." Maren nodded.

"Phout also asks about the boys? Are they here?"

"Bo," Maren says, and she turns to Phout. "Luk sai (son)—America…University." Then Maren added in English: "They are doing very well and wish they could be here with everyone." Phout, and the group, nodded with Malaithong's translation.

Phout turned toward me, held up one finger, and paused. She suddenly brightened: "Djozzzhhhh," she said hesitantly.

I cracked my smile wider to confirm her pronunciation. It was the first time in all our years of visits that she pronounced my name without being reminded.

She walked over and touched me lightly on one shoulder. She paused a moment, and looked like she was pulling up some deep secret: "Goo-ood moo-orning," she intoned roundly, despite the late hour. Phout looked around at everyone to show off a bit of English that we had practiced on a previous visit. Everyone laughed with her. She looked at me again—right into my eyes—and asked via Malaithong how my mother, who had visited four years earlier, was doing. I confirmed she was doing well and that she sent her greetings. Everyone nodded as Malaithong translated. Phout nodded—I could feel her say "Thank you for being here." Everything from Phout comes straight from the heart.

Phout reached for the plastic bags she had brought and started doling them out to people with quick, sharp instructions. Hamman smiled as he pulled several fried pig ears from one bag, and

Phout and Nang Tiip share a jar of lao hai, a fermented rice beverage.

he reached for the knife on his waist-belt to slice them for a shared appetizer. Another bag reveals several stark-white bamboo shoots and another held two halves of a long zucchini-like vegetable; Malaithong took them to the kitchen. Souksakone reached into a yellow bin set against the wall and pulled out two large Beer Lao bottles, and several glasses appeared. They were quickly filled and everyone reached. "Sokdee, sabaidee," we said as we toasted each other's company. "Good luck, good health."

The world has been a more gregarious place since July 10, 1970, the day Phout entered the world, born to Khamanee and Maikhom of Xam Tai, both of whom still live locally. Her quiet mother still weaves with incredible precision, and her cheerful father, a farmer and important spiritual leader, performed the role of the mophone at a recent Baci ceremony in our honor.

Phout started weaving and helping her mother with dyeing when she was six years old, and today she admits that from the beginning

Phout, Souksakone, and Malaithong celebrate at Phout's son Jai's wedding.

she loved to sit at the loom and create. Due to her talent, dedication and tenacity, she was excused from regular fieldwork that everyone else in the family was obligated to perform; her time spent at the loom provided a better service for the family. She grew up playing with best friends Souksakone and Malaithong, and stayed in school until early adolescence. However, since economic times were tough in the immediate post-war years, she had to turn to full-time textile work when she was twelve. She is proud that she has been able to afford to educate her children through the university level because of her weaving and business talent.

Unlike many others in the region, Phout's mother remained (and still remains) devoted to dyeing her silk and cotton textiles with traditional, natural dyes. Phout remembers experimenting with the cheap chemical dyes that were imported from Vietnam, and how her mother and she hated, in particular, the dye that turned her hands a putrid, glowing green for a week. Plus, Phout adds, chemical dyes can be used only once, whereas her natural dyes can be saved and reused many times.

Phout met her husband, Bounphan, at the loom. He was a soldier, and he would visit her when she sat at her loom so they could "flirt the hours away." They married in 1988 and became the parents of two daughters and a son (as is often the case, one child, the son, is not Phout's birth-child, but rather a nephew she raised from childhood). The eldest daughter, Phouang, is an avid weaver and helps run the silk business from her home in the capital, Vientiane. She and her husband, Nan (who has learned English), have also become good friends of ours. They have built a new house and bought a car, and have treated Phout to her first grandchild. Phout's second son, Deng, is just now completing his studies at the university in Vientiane, and we all celebrated together at the wedding of her older son, Jai, in Xam Tai in March, 2016. [We are deeply saddened to add that Bounphan, Phout's husband of twenty-eight years, passed away from cancer in June, 2016.]

In 2003, Phout, following the lead of her colleagues Souksakone and Lun, stepped into the business world and began dyeing silk and designing traditional textiles for the broader marketplace. On a shoestring budget and completely self-supporting, and with the inspiration of her spirited aunt Sukkhavit, Phout invested in local silk- and dye-work, committed to several of her template designs, and coordinated with several of the best local weavers to produce silks that she believed would be attractive in the developing tourist and international marketplace.

Phout is a workhorse, and is busy dawn to dusk, and even later, with any number of projects. She seems tireless, always ready to do the extra shift, whether it's staying up until dawn to get some skeins dyed to meet our travel deadline or washing dishes after an evening's celebration. She brings her contagious, upbeat energy and quick, ready laugh to every task.

Her dye-work is superb, although she admittedly bows to the breadth of knowledge that Souksakone maintains. Phout's jewel-tone purples and blues are particularly lush and delicious, and her rich browns and greens radiate warmth and depth.

She has collected, revised, and created an array of design templates, and her expertise in template design provides the foundation for our description of the khao nyeung, the design-template attached to the loom that both dictates and preserves the complex weaving design (pages 169-179). While Phout has several treasured traditional templates (such as her man-woman phaa sabai), she has also created her own unique patterns that she believes reflect the art of traditional design yet meet an aesthetic—and price point—that finds success in the urban marketplace.

She currently coordinates with and supplies her naturally-dyed silk to fifty weavers in Xam Tai and Meung Kuan Districts. Like Lun and Souksakone, she not only provides the materials and design template for the weavers working under her direction, she also sets a standard of quality and consistency that is required for sales in the urban market. We will explore this vital, modern role of managing traditional textiles and weavers in balance with the marketplace when we visit Souksakone (pages 152–57).

Perhaps Phout's greatest gift of all to us, however, beyond that of offering her open heart, is that she tells a great story. Not a day has gone by when we have been with Phout where we have not seen her peers sit back with eager smiles and let her charge into a spirited monologue. Even for those of us who know very little Lao (and in truth, Malaithong is usually laughing too hard to translate it all anyway), it is always a gifted performance.

All of Phout's cheer and optimism, all of her energy and spirit, all of her tireless desire to engage radiates from her and immerses everyone lucky to be near. As well, she has been central to our welcome in Xam Tai, and has been a vessel of information and detail about dyeing, template-making, weaving, and the marketplace. She is, simply, one of the most engaging and nourishing people we have ever met, and one can't help but be present in her presence.

## MAIKHOM OF XAM TAI

Maikhom takes some credit for Phout's exuberance and work ethic—she is her mother.

Born in Xam Tai in 1949 when it was only a small village of seventy homes, it was Maikhom's mother, Bee, who taught Maikhom to weave at age ten. Maikhom remembers her childhood fondly, and laughs when she recalls riding water buffalo across the river and swimming in the Nam Xam.

Her face grows graver when she recalls the war. For ten years she lived in the forest under camouflaged lean-to shelters. She remembers times when food was scarce, and farming could only be done under the cover of nightfall.

At age eighteen, in the middle of the war, she married Khamanee, who was four years her junior. She now laughs at the challenges of having a husband so young, and how she had to be very patient and do many of the house tasks in their early years together. Today Khamanee is a handsome, successful village leader. He is also a mophone, a spiritual leader who chants and leads the Baci healing ceremony. Together they have a son and a daughter (Phout), and they also adopted another girl who was born to a cousin.

Maikhom learned from her mother the art of silk raising, dyeing, and weaving, and she is proud of having passed both her skills and work ethic to Phout. She also affirms for us that she was, and still is, very good at "seeing colors and patterns."

Maikhom's weaving is still meticulous at age sixty-seven, and although she confesses that she is slowing down these days, the quality of her artistry merits the highest praise.

"I am happy with my life," she smiles. "I am very proud of my daughter and all the young weavers in Xam Tai. I hope everyone will keep weaving and do good things with their lives."

# Four. Textile Creation

*The idea for a pattern is not the design itself. The desire for friendship is not friendship. Only careful attention can build such meaning and reward.*

*Our life is created with and by others. Our textures. Our colors. Our motifs, both bold and hidden.*

*Whom did I meet today? What was shared and honored? What was created?*

*Or did I miss a swift pass of the shuttle, a thread of possibility and potential....*

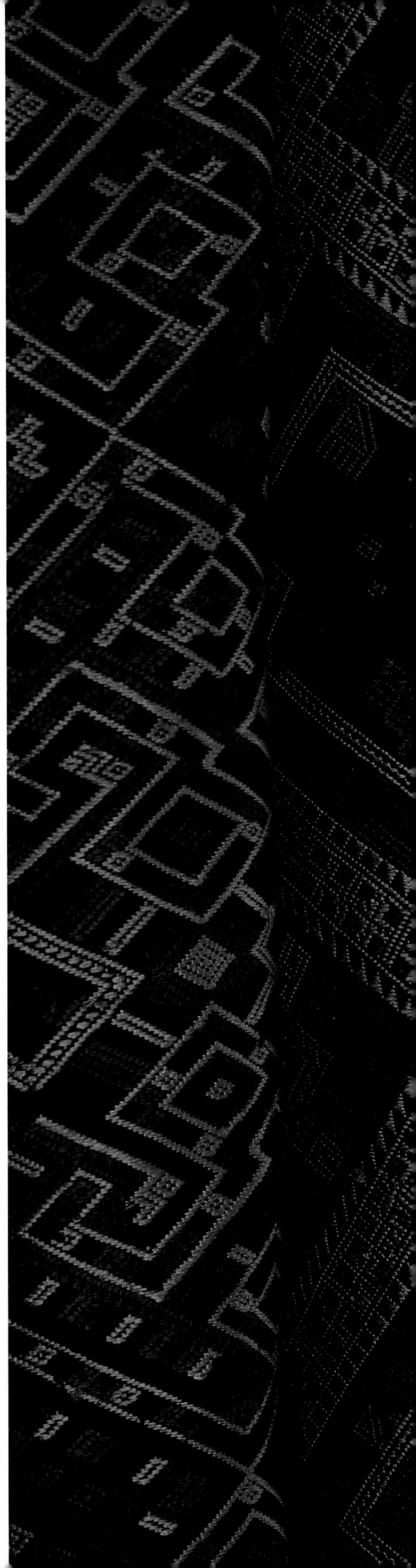

CHAPTER NINETEEN

# The Art of Xam Tai Design and Motifs

The ancestors of all of us endured, cursed, and personalized the external forces that interfered with their well-being, and all human traditions create forms and symbols to represent the trials, fears, and hopes that define the human experience.

The miraculous iconography of Xam Tai's textiles were borne from, and continue to be shaped by, the rich traditions and stories that have emerged from the diverse and fertile imaginations and experiences of the regional weavers, healers, and other storytellers. Fantastical creatures, jungle animals, plants and seeds, rainbows and candles, boats, horses, rice, the sun and the moon—all representations that seek to connect us with the spiritual in the quest for well-being—twist and roil and march and hide and dance and shine in outrageous geometric complexity.

It is a tangled world where Escher meets Dali, where shape and color jump and play and surprise, and where an ancient past reveals its ornate relevance to the twenty-first century.

The manifestation of a textile-oriented art form that represents a spiritual tradition is not unique to Lao-Tai culture, but the breadth of member participation, the intri cacy of the iconography, and the fundamental expressions of form are unique.

Opposite: Shoulder cloths show intricate motifs and brilliant combinations of natural dyes.

Ellison Findly describes the elaborate complexity of the regional textiles as a "text" that can be "read," or interpreted. The decisions made in producing a cloth regarding materials, dye methods, and specific design elements are the weaver's "grammar" and "vocabulary." The effort to generate the textile and grant it meaning, whether for healing, protection, or facilitating a life event such as a funeral, is the "syntax." She describes the language as fluid, with a virtually infinite array of variations that are "capable of carrying many and subtly different meanings at the same time."

Xam Tai's unique fusion of animist and Buddhist traditions reveals itself in this visual language. In general, motifs born from animist traditions symbolically focus on accessing and placating the world of spirits and the afterlife. This world is full of strange blends of creatures, and the human efforts to illuminate and gain access and influence over the unknown. These cloths often have elements of asymmetry and are woven in highly complex mirror-image patterns that easily hide the motifs and deceive the eye.

Motifs born from Buddhist traditions generally emphasize the natural world and today's real life; the forms tend to be geometric and the aesthetic emphasizes the beauty of symmetry and balance. Patterning tends to be repetitive, and the motifs are of the physical world.

Xam Tai's textiles lean to the animist, yet are not hesitant to embrace traditional Buddhist iconography. Which makes sense: unlike the rest of Laos, this particular region has a proud Tai Daeng (animist) tradition and, geographically, has been more isolated from the Buddhist influences than the western Lao provinces and Thailand.

As such, Xam Tai's emphasis on the animist's peculiar, fantastical creature-spirits tends to intrigue the eyes and hearts of western textile enthusiasts, and this iconography helps distinguish Xam Tai–style textiles from those designed elsewhere in Laos.

What, then, does this mix of motifs that are cohabiting on these silk textiles mean? What is the intention of a motif or design? For an answer, one would have to ask the weaver, or the person requesting that the pattern be woven. Of course, one may also ask the person using the textile, or even the

Draught ngueak or two-headed baby ngueak with scales. Middle: Intertwined ngueak laying eggs. Bottom: Curly-tailed ngueak.

person looking at the phaa sabai hanging on the wall of our home in Eugene, Oregon. Meaning isn't solely derived in creation, nor is meaning destined to be static. Its only requirement is participation of sense and mind.

Findly offers those of us trying to gain clarity a bit of consolation:

"Although we are able to identify various patterns with the help of the weavers, there is no real systematic pattern of symbolism. Images are viewed and understood in many ways…and it is clear that applied meanings adapt to immediate circumstances: e.g. what's remembered about history, what materials are available, what's seen in the environment, what the local familial situation is, and what the interviewer is thought to want to hear. While we try then to give an understanding of a certain process or design element, we find that weavers have many things to say about it, and that this 'multi-valency' is an important aspect of how a given textile fits into real life."

Thus, one final element is revealed to dampen the romance of textile meaning and spiritual and cultural continuity: today's weavers are, by and large, either making clothing for their own family (pretty rare) or weaving textiles for the marketplace. That is, they're either saving money or making money. Not that making a living isn't supporting a vital quest. But the purpose of weaving, and the decision to spend time at the loom, is often, here in the twenty-first century, decidedly pragmatic.

Perhaps something has been lost.

As discussed earlier, at one time certain design elements and motifs in daily-wear and ceremonial textiles indicated specific cultural and familial lineage; this use of textiles as an "identifier" provided a strong sense of cohesion in past generations when tribal groups were more isolated and politics more local. But this identifying characteristic of design no longer holds, at least among the people and villages we know. Modern communications, transportation, markets, and geopolitics have all played a role in reducing isolation and unifying the people as citizens of Laos.

Not that this diminishes the quality, style, or power of the woven art form. Indeed, loosening cultural restrictions on traditional textile design has allowed some textile artists—Lun, Phout, and Souksakone among them—to push the form to attract a broader audience in multiple markets.

List-makers can place Xam Tai's textile motifs into five categories: mythological creatures and spirits, living animals, plants and seeds, the environment, and human-made objects. In that first category, four traditional mythological creature-motifs (and their many variations) are particularly common and profound: the *ngueak/naak* (river serpent), the *hong/saang/siho* (bird/elephant), the *khon buhaan* (ancestor spirit), and the *phii nyak* (giant spirit). Textiles that use these mythic creatures have traditionally tended to have a "transformative" function, and are meant to exert a power to generate a benefit.

## Ngueak/Naak ("River Serpent")

The most common motif found in Xam Tai's textiles, by a good stretch, is the *ngueak*, a "river serpent." These legless dragons, which weave and wrap their narrow, angular bodies across all styles of textiles, usually have a triangular single-eyed head attached to a long zig-zag that stretches horizontally across a textile. The end of a ngueak may reveal a tail, or perhaps another ngueak's head.

Animist Tai Daeng legend holds that the powerful ngueak live in tunnels under the villages by the river. They are fierce and powerful, and protect villagers from evil spirits. The ngueak carry responsibilities for bringing rain for drinking, bathing, and farming, and are known to protect the complex, vital irrigation networks. Big rainstorms are said to be the result of angry ngueaks thrashing their tails; others say that storms are ngueaks playfully twisting their tails as they joust each other in fun. In myth they can take on human form, and several tales speak of ngueaks carrying on love affairs with humans.

Unlike traditional four-legged Chinese dragons (in Lao, *mangkorn*), the legless ngueak embrace female energy—fierce, protective, loyal, strong. They are not to be "messed with," and are known to tip over boats and devour victims from the "inside out."

Rich, intricate motifs in this old textile woven by Souksakone's great-grandmother delight and challenge the eye.

They identify with the color red, and ancient tradition holds that anyone wearing red outside of a ceremony is being disrespectful of the ngueak's power. Even today, some elders will take off any red clothing before crossing a river for fear (or perhaps out of tradition) that an angry ngueak might capsize the boat and drown the blasphemer.

That's the river serpent of animist lore.

Born from the Buddhist tradition (and out of Hindu/Indic traditions) is the

Top left: Saang hong with khon buhaan on its back. Top right: Two-headed saang hong, pregnant with curly-tailed ngueaks. Bottom: Siho, pregnant with ngueaks, with trunks that become ngueaks.

*naga*, a revered giant serpent who makes its first appearance sheltering the Buddha under its hood for thirty days when the evil goddess Mara sent a great storm. In the Lao language, the Pali word "*naga*" is transliterated as "*naak*," and one is apt to hear both pronunciations in talking with weavers who uphold a Buddhist interpretation.

Naak are followers of the Buddha, and thus do not carry quite the deliberate fierceness of the ngueak. As followers of the Buddha, naak practice the eight moral precepts that protect the followers of Buddha. Naak are generally thought of as benevolent, but still powerful; they command reverence. Buddhist temples often have naak painted or carved on the temple roofs and steps; they are a common motif on the shoulder cloths women wear to the local Buddhist temple.

This dual interpretation of the ngueak and naak is typical of the unique blend of traditions and belief in the Xam Tai region. Those who lean toward animist ancestry and perspective lean toward the ngueak as an explanation for the motif; those who lean toward Buddhist theology are more apt to describe the motif as a naak. In truth, most weavers seem to use the words interchangeably.

There are many dozens of variations of the motif. Some naak have rainbow-like stripes stretched across their bellies, and are said to be pregnant, and symbols of fertility. Some have crests on their heads; others are entwined and said to be mating. There are two-headed naak and naak with bent, hooked, crossed, coiled, or curly tails—or tails, if you follow them far enough, that turn into an elephant's trunk. There are "boxes of naak" and "vines of naak." There are even ngueak that form a boat to help the animist healer to the "world of spirits," or a Buddhist healer to the location of a patient's lost khoune.

The ngueak/naak is a creature, and motif, to be respected, as is evident in these two tales from *Weaving Cloth, Weaving Na-*

*gas* by Viengkham Nanthavongdouangsy.

This first tale is from the animist Tai Daeng tradition:

### Mai Faa and the Pretty Girl

Once upon a time there was a poor family of a Mother, Father and a beautiful little Daughter living in a small village. The Mother and Daughter grew mulberry bushes to feed silkworms. The silkworms had to be fed for two full moons before they made their cocoons, and they stayed inside for a long time and hatched only once a year. So the family named this silk Mai Faa (literally, "silk year").

Then the mother reeled the faa silk yarn out of the cocoon. Mai Faa was very strong and very hard to break. The mother gave Mai Faa to the Father, and the Father made it into a fishing net. After finishing, the Father gave the net to the Daughter who then went fishing. The daughter carried with her a basket of embroidery equipment such as yarn, fabric, and a knife, and she embroidered her Sinh while she fished.

After a while there came a noise from the river. She looked down and saw a long Ngueak caught by the net.

"Young girl, please help me! I am in pain! The net is very strong. It is stronger than any net I have ever seen!" cried the Ngueak.

The daughter listened to the Ngueak's pleading and felt pity for it. She took her knife and began to cut the net. She tried hard but the knife could not cut the yarn. Then she tried again while singing a song.

"La ni noi, La ni neu, La ni nut. Cut this yarn to the next. Cut the next to the near. Please! Please yarns, leave the Ngueak."

As soon as the song ended, the yarn released the Ngueak. The Ngueak was very happy and invited the Daughter to visit his town under the river. At first the daughter refused but the Ngueak asked her again and again to give him a chance to return her kindness.

The Daughter went down to the Ngueak's town and met with the parents of the young Ngueak who were the King and Queen of the town. The King and the Queen listened to the story and were very grateful to the Daughter for allowing their son to survive. Before leaving the Ngueak's town, the King and Queen gave the Daughter a couple of bags. The first bag contained white ginger, and the second contained yellow ginger. The Daughter returned home with the two bags, and when she opened them the white ginger turned to silver and the yellow turned to gold. Since then the poor family was wealthy and lived together happily.

Ever since that day, when people travel by river, they like to have the Mai Faa yarn tied to their wrists to protect them from the danger of the water snake.

This second tale is from the Buddhist Lao Loum tradition:

### The Weaving Shuttle of the King's Daughter

A long time ago there was a charming Kingdom by a big river. The King of this Kingdom had a very beautiful daughter. She was not only famous for her beauty but also famous for her weaving skills as well. She was very good at fine and delicate weaving, and the patterns of her clothes were astonishing.

The reputation of the King's daughter was known amongst people both inside and outside the territory. Many young men came to see her and asked to marry her, but she refused. Her fame crossed the land to a young Naak who lived in the "Badan," the Naak Kingdom below the big river. The Naak could not stand waiting to see her, so he turned himself into a white cock with a big red crest, then came up to watch her while she was weaving under her house on stilts.

When the Naak saw the King's daughter he fell in love with her so badly that every day he had to turn himself into the white cock with the red crest to go look at her. One day while she was weaving, the white cock used his strong, sharp beak to pick up her shuttle and run away. The King's daughter ran after the white cock and her shuttle. She ran, and ran, and ran until she came to the big river. The shuttle didn't stop there, so she swam into the river and dived to its bottom. She saw the shuttle fall into a deep hole, and she followed it deeper and deeper into the hole and reached the Naak Kingdom.

Because of his love and wish to marry the King's daughter, the Naak was very afraid to let her see his Naak features, so he turned himself into a good looking man. He also asked the other Naak in the Kingdom to turn themselves into human beings, too.

When the King's daughter saw the good looking man she fell in love with him whole-heartedly and was happy to marry him. However, the King's daughter was very sad when she thought of her father, who she would miss if she stayed with her husband. On the other hand, if she asked her husband to live with her in her Kingdom then the Naak could not stay alive. So both of them cried, and cried, and cried for three days and three nights, and their tears filled up the river and almost flooded her father's Kingdom. All the Naak were sad because of their love and wanted to help. So they found a deer and used a spell to turn it into the King's daughter, then sent it back to live with the King as usual. Unfortunately, this "replacement" daughter soon became sick and died. The King, believing she was his real daughter, grieved deeply.

The real King's daughter learned about her father's sadness and became very upset and wanted to visit him. She pleaded with her husband to take her up to her Kingdom and the Naga felt pity for his wife and agreed to bring her together with the other Naak to visit the King.

The King was so happy to see his daughter again as he listened to her story that he didn't mind having a Naak as a son-in-law. He invited people from all over the Kingdom for a welcome ceremony for his daughter and son-in-law. To prepare for the ceremony people enjoyed cooking food, but while they were cooking herbs and grilling chilies, the smell of the chilies flew into the nose and eyes of the Naak. The Naak could not stand the spicy smell of the chilies, so they had to excuse themselves and ask leave of the King, who brought the daughter back to live happily in the Naak Kingdom, leaving behind the King and his people to enjoy their normal lives.

Since then, whenever there is a heavy storm, people believe that a Naak is getting angry and blowing the wind from its mouth. They burn chilies to make a spicy smell, believing this will help to stop the strong wind by causing the Naga to move away.

---

## Hong/Saang ("Bird/Elephant")

The counter to the female, protective nature of the ngueak and naak is found in the hong, a mythical creature that again emerges from both animist and Buddhist traditions and is said to hold male energy. It manifests itself in a variety of representative forms and is commonly found in ceremonial textiles.

The hong's primary form is that of a bird, and it is representative of both freedom and the entry (birth) and exit (death) of humans from our world. Unlike the ngueak, its realm is the sky and the heavens. In Tai Daeng lore, its belly is a rainbow, and as such its motif can declare itself simply as multi-colored stripes on a sinh, mosquito net border, or funeral banner.

The hong also manifests itself as surrealistic dual-species creatures such as a saang hong (literally, "elephant-bird"), a bizarre tiny-clawed, two-footed long-trunked hybrid, or as a siho, an elephant-lion with four thick legs, a trunk, and a long tail. Its elephant-like manifestations are symbolic of strength and political power, traditional dominant realms of the male. This odd dichotomy of a spirit representing both something that flies and travels freely yet is grounded on earth with a weight of authority is just a given.

There are a variety of strange manifestations: siho with two heads, giant-headed hong with minute bodies, and saang (elephants) whose trunks become ngueak, and ngueak whose heads are saang.

It gets odder: The symbology of the hong extends to images of boats as well.

Repeated down the center of this textile, Khon buhaan in a huea hong, also called a "wax naga" boat. An ancestor spirit is in a temple with a candelabra on the roof.

Shamans, in healing ceremonies, symbolically utilize a huea hong—a "hong boat"—that can transport ill-serving spirits "out" during a ceremony and then harbor good spirits back "in." This boat motif often has gables lined with candles that help light the way. The huea hong is also associated with transporting souls to the afterlife. Cheesman points out that boats, in legend, can also be manifestations of ngueaks, and today the boats that race on the river during celebrations, also called huea hong, have carved bird heads on the prow and serpent scales painted on the sides. Could the huea hong then symbolize the merging of the female and male spirit that, within each of us, seeks to find a healthy balance between nurturance and discipline, and between looking to the past and reaching for the future?

The imaginations and spirits of a hundred generations of weavers and shamans have been at play and at work, and trying to untangle the variations and interpretations in a world that has stewed so long is as challenging and futile as organizing one's dreams.

## Khon Buhaan ("Ancestor Spirit")

Often on a textile one will find a single standing person-image, a khon buhaan (khon is the human figure, buhaan means ancestor), with arms held high, each hand extending several fingers. Sometimes the figure is represented with male genitalia, but today's textiles, especially those being woven for the marketplace, are, shall we say, left "unstemmed." Often the motif stands on the back of a saang or siho, or can be found inside a "candle room" (haung tian) set on a huea hong.

The khon buhaan is a power that can travel between the lower world of the ngueak, the middle world of the saang, and the sky-world of the hong. Indeed, our ancestors have much to teach us about the breadth of experience and the art of well-being.

For this motif, we share our own story:

"Siho?" Maren queried of Bounkeo, pointing to the silver-threaded motif of a mythological elephant-lion woven in the shaman's cloth spread on the table.

Bounkeo paused a moment. "Bo," he said. No. He looked directly at Maren and waggled a finger. "Siho bo. Saang chou." Mythological elephant-lion no. Regular elephant yes.

Maren flipped through our dog-eared Lao-Tai textile book and found a nearly identical image that identified the figure as a siho of the Tai Daeng tradition. Yet here was Bounkeo, who is Tai Daeng, saying that this motif was a creature of the natural world, and not of myth.

Maren pointed to the human-like figure on the elephant's back. "Khon buhaan?" she asked. Ancestor figure? She posed for a moment like a khon buhaan herself, her legs squat wide and her arms held outward, with her palms open and fingers pointing up. She pouted her lips outward for effect, her face reminding me of the fierce "Woman of the Woods" masks of the Haida people of western Canada.

Bounkeo stared at Maren's pose for a moment and burst out laughing. "Chou, chou, chou," he finally squeaked out. Yes, yes, yes. "Khon buhaan!" He turned to me, gathered himself with false bravado, and then squatted just as Maren had posed. He waved both his upright hands toward himself. "Khoy (I) khon buhaan," he growled, and we all laughed.

Maren pointed again to the "khon buhaan" figure in the book. "Ani (Is this) khon buhaan?" she asked.

Bounkeo suddenly looked serious. "Bo, bo." he said, "Pou saai." It's a man.

We looked to Malaithong to help us out. She exchanged a couple of sentences with Bounkeo and said: "Bounkeo says this is an elephant trainer on the back of an elephant. He is teaching the elephant to do work."

Maren frowned and then traced the small diamond shape at the base of the motif in the book with her finger. One of our academic sources spoke of female ancestor spirits, and had provided a photo of the traditional khon buhaan motif with a diamond between the legs–a symbol of female anatomy. In our own research, this seemed relevant given that the regional silk-weaving tradition included both the patrilineal Tai Daeng with the matrilineal Lao Loum ethnic groups. Further, traditional shaman-healers may be either women or men. We had wondered if khon buhaan could be men or women. However, now Bounkeo was saying that this motif was of an elephant with its male mahout.

"Phou nying?" Maren asked. Woman? And she again outlined the diamond between the legs of the figure.

Bounkeo uttered "Bo, bo, bo" under his breath, and then said a couple lines to Malaithong.

Malaithong laughed. "Bounkeo says

that women never get on an elephant. It is a man's place."

We've no doubt that the published expert was told by sources that a diamond between the legs of a "khon buhaan" figure indicated it was female. Was that source following another set of traditions unknown to Bounkeo and the people we know? Or were we hearing the "modern day" now speaking, as distinct from the "traditional, timeless way" of ancestors?

In a world where cultural transmission is of an oral and symbolic nature, human understandings of the universe gain a fluid and dynamic quality; as such, the ancestral conceptions of the interconnectedness of nature, spirit, and humanity becomes open to pragmatic re-interpretation even though the act of transmission itself—the process of textile creation—remains vital and consistent.

Whole image of a phii naak over an orange two-headed pregnant ngeuak.

## Phii Nyak ("Giant Spirit")

The most terrifying, and also protective, spirit-motif is that of the phii nyak, or "giant spirit." This spirit carries a centered rhomb-shaped head, often crested and one-eyed, with wide arms that spiral outward and resemble the coiled tail of a ngueak. We see these images primarily on children's blankets (phaa tuum), where the motif is often starkly formed in indigo against a white background. Phii nyak can also be found on funeral cloths, healing cloths, and door curtains. It has a protective "doorkeeper" function, and, again like the ngueak, is both feared and worshipped.

Legends place the terrifying phii nyak in the forest, where he laughs as long as there is light in the sky. They can stand straight and tall—their long arms, uncoiled, can reach way out—and are said to grab children who wander into the forest. They bite their victim at the base of the neck, with one lip covering the face and the other covering the body down to the chest, and then crack open the skull and drink the person's blood. Phii nyak are said also to be able to eat your spirit (khoune). However, they only seek people with bad intentions (or perhaps children who wander away without permission), and their fierceness, once enshrined in a textile, can be harnessed to protect people who are upstanding or innocent.

## Real-World Motifs

Textiles used for daily functions, such as door curtains, mosquito net borders, and pillows, will tend toward motifs that represent "real-world" items which may, or may not, have traditional spiritual weight.

Real-world motifs may not seem as deliciously dreamlike or romantically spiritual, but merging the mythological with the real world brings the senses to light. The mysterious and magical thus become mixed with the known and predictable; the barriers between past and present dissolve, and an ageless truth can be touched.

Real-world motifs fall into four categories: living animals, plants, the natural environment, and human-made objects.

Elephants, snakes, deer, frogs, horses, gibbons, silkworms, crabs, chickens, peacocks, and real birds (called nok, not hong) can all inhabit and grant symbolic meaning to a weaver's creation. A motif's meaning in such case is usually symbolic of something pragmatic: a rooster on a door curtain helps a family wake up. A pair of butterflies might reinforce harmony between spouses.

Plant motifs most often decorate borders or backgrounds, and the shapes include a variety of flowers, fiddlehead ferns, fruits, coconut fronds, rice plants, and an array of different-textured seeds. Gourd seeds are common, as one Tai Daeng myth has humans originally being born from such. The one plant motif we do occasionally find as a central symbol is the "Tree of Life." With its roots in the earth and branches in the heavens, this Buddhist-inspired motif connects the two realms of the worlds and helps in healing ceremonies.

The environment that surrounds Xam Tai is also ripe for conjuring images. There are motifs that represent mountains, rivers, clouds, and lightning; there are suns, moons, and stars.

Finally, the human-made objects, many of them "tools" to help a shaman with his or her goal, are common motifs: boats, lanterns, candles, hooks, keys, and ladders. House gable and temple motifs may stretch over and protect their dwellers.

Xam Tai's textiles are woven in the dynamic and changing world. Meaning can be layered and personal, yet it is still reliant upon—even bound—by tradition and form.

Real-world images of roosters and other animals often appear in door curtains and sinhs.

Findly writes: "Textiles as mythic worlds, then, are not necessarily consistent, and it is this inconsistency that makes them utterly human."

CHAPTER TWENTY

# Ban Tao Sushi

Our saungtheaw, a pick-up-style public "bus" with two hard benches in the bed, finally emerges from the narrow rutted jungle track that had followed the tumbling Nam Xam for an hour, and we lurch to a stop in front of Ban Tao's sole store. Our family of three (myself, Maren and Zall, as Ari now has college responsibilities) along with Malaithong and several others traveling from Xam Tai stretch the kinks from our jarred bones and, seeking shade from the close and humid sun, huddle in the shade of a scraggly papaya tree. A half-dozen local adults, and perhaps fifteen kids, all crowd close. It had been a couple of years, we are told, since anyone remembers falang visiting their town.

The store sells canned and dried goods as well as Chinese-made tools and plastics. Several varieties of potato-chip-like snacks in bright foil packets wait for attention. A fridge—and electricity, although sporadic, has only recently reached Ban Tao—proudly displays cold cans of Pepsi and bottles of Beer Lao and water. A few baskets of fresh vegetables and jungle fruits sit in front, seeking customers. A three-pound iguana, with a trickle of blood on its alert face, is leashed with a rope to a wooden post—no, one won't find fresher meat (and guess what Malaithong's family had for dinner that night).

We have traveled to Ban Tao because it is renowned for its sericulture. For generations, this small village of perhaps 200 people has been central to raising the highest-quality silk required by the weavers of Xam Tai.

The elected head of Ban Tao immediately appears, and Malaithong introduces our family. He knows the Xam Tai friends who have traveled with us, for most are dyers and weavers involved in the business, and not just the artisan, side of the trade. He nods and says he is honored that we would come to their village, but he is sad that we have come during the monsoon season, as this was not a time for harvesting the silk—they keep just enough silkworms going to maintain their "breeding stock" for the spring and fall growing seasons. But he would be honored to show us what he could, and to explain the process to us.

He has some quick words with a young man, who then dashes off down the road. In a few moments, we would realize that he darted off to facilitate a demonstration of the silk-reeling process even if it was not silk-reeling season.

He leads us, and the growing contingent of curious kids, to a small thatch-roofed house and immediately directs a group of young people to start a small fire. He was determined to show his special guests the full sericulture process. Smoke soon fills the now-crowded room; ten, fifteen, twenty

Opposite: Main street, Ban Tao. Below: Curious onlookers check out the visitors.

Silkworms grow to 10,000 times their starting size in a month.

people crowd in. Zall, eager to escape both the crowd and billowing smoke, pulls out a frisbee and a gaggle of boys rushes out to play in the dirt-track street.

Some silk cocoons appear and an elder woman, who was obviously now in charge of the production, quickly sets up a pot of water to boil and pulls out a set of long sticks that helps her handle the cocoons. Maren wears a full smile and a bead of sweat hangs on her nose; Malaithong is trying to translate for three simultaneous talkers; a baby starts to cry. The grandmother sits down at the fire and the crowd pulls back a bit. Wielding two long chopsticks, she demonstrates how one takes a worm's now-boiled cocoon and delicately pulls from the tiny, papoose-like bundle strands of exquisite thread that has been the treasure of royalty for millennia. We have seen the procedure before, but it is important for our relationship with these kind people that they demonstrate their full expertise.

An hour later we are led to another home. In the shade under the elevated floor, behind the fencing that keeps the roving chickens and ducks out, are trays of tiny silkworms devouring fresh mulberry leaves. The continuing "crop" of silk is being carefully nurtured.

Our Xam Tai friend, Phout, who had disappeared an hour earlier, finds us and announces that a late lunch is ready, and we brave the sun and return to the head person's home.

Three tables have been pushed together and before we even reach the table Lun's husband, Bounkeo, rushes over, slightly flushed. He grabs my arm and pulls me in ahead of Maren and Zall and points to the table. He nods emphatically, grabs a pair of chopsticks and reaches out to snatch a small cube of fresh-filleted raw catfish from the plate in front of him. With a flourish of ceremony he dips the morsel into a small dish of gray soy sauce and holds it up to my mouth. He shares a big grin, eyebrows raised.

A wave of alarm shoots up and through my nose, and I close my eyes tightly to endure the exploding rush. I catch my breath, blink a tear—finally rediscover my equanimity—only to find a smiling Bounkeo, and a few others, laughing. I take a deep breath and issue a slow, high-pitched emphatic: "Wa-sa-bi."

Everyone laughs and a short glass of Beer Lao is placed into my hands. On the table next to the fish is a familiar green tube of Thai-made "S & W Brand Wasabi." It never fails to rattle us how close the modern is to what can feel so remote.

The ten or so of us all feast on the delicate sushi (perhaps going a bit easier on the wasabi), and then three big bowls of fish soup spiced with lemongrass are brought out to share. Plates of slightly-bitter morning glory and two steaming bowls of bamboo shoots arrive. Baskets of sticky rice are passed around, along with several small bowls of spicy djaow, the thick chili-gar-

We enjoy a full lunch, freshly prepared, in the town of Ban Tao with friends.

lic-ginger dip for finger-rolled balls of rice and bamboo spears.

The head of the village reappears from inside his private portion of the house with a large bottle of what had originally contained Russian vodka. The bottle must hold two liters, and the original label had been carefully maintained. It did look particularly regal.

Once assured he had everyone's eyes, he picks up the single shot glass, gives a brief speech that Malaithong translates, with each noun at a higher pitch: "Best of wishes, and good health, and good business, and good luck, and to friendship." It seems virtually all toasts and ceremonial words reduce to these lines. The single glass circles the room, with each recipient sharing a nod with the group as they toss the shot down. Everyone partakes, including Zall.

This deep-amber shot is warm and smooth, fuzzy in my mouth. A numbing tingle spreads from my lips over my tongue and down my throat.

The bottle is shared again, one shot each, and again the head person starts with a few words and a lift of the glass in the direction of Maren, myself, and Zall. Again a numbing, this time from my scalp to my toes. My tongue can barely feel my lips. "Sep," I say to no one in particular, "Sep lai." Delicious, very delicious. The host nods and I reach to examine the bottle.

Oh-so-fresh catfish sushi and wasabi!

Inside the bottle, underneath a few sticks of some seasoning wood, are the corpses of an army of large "bumblers." As in hundreds of partially-to-totally decomposing and decomposed bumble bees. Alive, each is perhaps an inch (2.5 cm) long and, I swear, creates a wind when it goes by. They have a powerful and intimidating buzz, and are feared less for their aggressiveness than for their bumbling clumsiness. In a jar of homemade rice whiskey, the power of that buzz absolutely remains.

After the meal we all stretch out on the cooler cement floor. Three of the men, heads on dense seating pillows, appear to fall asleep.

The village head excuses himself—he has to attend an important function in recognition of a local policeman's promotion. Malaithong also excuses herself to spend some personal time with an aunt and uncle who live in town (what town doesn't she have relatives in?). She must be exhausted to have Lao and English grammar jabbering simultaneously in her head, and we've always greatly appreciated the fact that Malaithong has never hesitated to set aside personal time to "clear the noise." It also forces us to practice our Lao language skills and hone our skills for developing connections without the benefit of fluency.

The room is quiet, just the turn of an extra-slow fan. Zall stretches out and seems to melt into the ever-so-slightly-cooler vinyl floor. It is hot. Maren's eyes are shut.

Escaping into the bright heat outside, I turn my head toward some loud pop music blaring from speakers up on the hillside. Some man—is that the village head?—is up at a home on the side of the hill, waving for me to join. Then another dozen faces peer over a bamboo balcony, and a young man and woman, with big smiles, rush down to my side and insist, with a flurry of words, that I join the party.

I'm handed a short glass of Beer Lao, and, following local tradition, I offer a nod of thanks and toss it down in one gulp (ahh—a cold one on a hot day can be a good thing!). I hand back the glass only to be handed another a moment later, and then a tray of unidentifiable fried meat chunks, I'll guess either dog or deer, is offered, and a plate of bananas and some other plum-like fruit, and then another glass of beer.

The Lao pop music—what I believe may be the same three songs playing over and over—is turned up. The gentleman getting the promotion, who looks no older than sixteen, throws his arm around me and says something in a loud voice and everyone, including me, laughs. More toasts, more beers and then a giant jackfruit is cut open and shared. The village head comes to my side and over the din of the sappy pop song and the laughter offers what seems to be a more serious-minded toast. He looks me straight in the eye, and drinks the short glass himself. Immediately he refills the glass and hands it to me. I offer, in English, what I hope sounds like a humble thank-you and then lift a toast to our shared moment of friendship and joy and indulgence. Everyone cheers. Translator, schmanslator.

An hour later, just as the promotion party is dispersing, Maren and Zall, each with several textiles in their arms, track me down. Apparently, they'd spent the last half hour looking at some older silks that the chief's wife had brought out of a closet, including a fifty-year-old silk coffin cover and an old used mosquito net border still with its original handspun indigo-dyed cotton side panels. Maren looks at me, one eyebrow cocked.

Petanque finishes out the day. Here, Phout's husband, Bounphan, and Josh make a team.

"It's all right," I stammer a bit sloppily. "I'll just take a quick catnap on the ride back...."

The next day, back at our accommodations in Xam Tai, the head of Ban Tao suddenly appears. He has a friendly business relationship with our hostess, Souksakone, at whose guesthouse we are staying.

We share some food and drink, and there is again the traditional exchange of beer–even at 10 am–although not enough to alter the day's trajectory of tasks. Malaithong translates that the most important reason he is visiting is to play a game of petanque with me, one-on-one, on the small court set up in Souksakone's front courtyard. Malaithong's eyes and tone inform me that his invitation is formal; we had not yet had our full time together.

I can't remember who won. But we shared and enjoyed a half hour of each other's company. We laughed at our errors, cheered at our luck. We shared attention and affection. We smiled and chatted in our respective languages, the content of the words secondary to the bond recognized.

The bonds that create friendships and respect and purpose need only to be acknowledged to be empowered.

CHAPTER TWENTY-ONE

# Silkworms and the Art of Sericulture

Today, in 2016, Ban Tao carries an air of success; homes are tidy and the dirt road is swept clean. The silk production and weaver artisans who live here seem confident they can earn a modest but steady flow of income. Many dozens of looms are set up under the traditional stilted homes, and through the open doors of the cooler cement-block homes a wanderer can see more looms.

Reliable electricity from the national power grid is a recent arrival. Cell phone towers are up and the main street has two streetlamps to help the evening stroller. The 20 km road from Xam Tai wanders the narrow canyon of the Xam River to Ban Tao; it is currently being graded and widened, a daunting task given the steep jungle slopes and summer's monsoon rains. It will hasten the pace of change, no doubt.

Opposite: Silkworm moths hatch out of their cocoons and immediately find a mate. Above: Fresh leaves of the mulberry bush.

About half the homes in Ban Tao are newer cement block, and half are the traditional wood and bamboo homes that stand on seven-foot stilts. The older-style homes look so appealing even if they do not offer respite in the heat of the day. They look more "of the land," and between the traditional second-floor porch and the benches that often beckon in the shade under a home, the old design seems to inspire people to gather—to join together and endure the day's heat—giving people the space to share.

Ducking under the beam that held up the stilted home, the home's owner leads us over to a dustier section, tucked up against some long-unused farm equipment. A crude rack of used boards and red brick create a simple set of deep shelves, upon which six loosely-woven bamboo baskets are arranged. The worn baskets are square on the bottom, about two feet (.6 m) wide with a ten-inch (25 cm) vertical rim. Each is covered by a grubby piece of cotton sheeting to protect the contents from harsh light; under that, a mosquito net assures protection from hungry pests.

Peeking under the sheeting and netting—careful, the owner alerts, flies are the enemy here!—one would be likely to find, in one form or another, a community of silkworms.

Perhaps it is summer, the warm and moldy monsoon season, and the thousands of silkworm eggs are pasted onto the inside of a well-used blue piece of tarp that is carefully folded and tucked into the basket. Perhaps it is a few weeks later, and the two-inch-long (6 cm) hundred-footed silkworms are clinging en masse to the edges of fresh green mulberry leaves, each nibbler carving its own small bay into the leaf.

Or perhaps it is a month later, and the soft, strong, protective cocoon is ready to reveal the inhabitant's transformation.

Surely, the first star of Xam Tai's textiles is the domesticated silkworm itself, *Bombyx mori*, nature's inspired spinner.

Chinese legend tells the tale of the

Empress Leizu, wife of the Yellow Emperor Huang Ti, who, one day in 2640 BC, was enjoying the shade of a white mulberry tree when a caterpillar's cocoon fell into her hot tea. In an effort to remove the cocoon, the empress noticed that it had begun to unravel into spiderweb-thin strands with a beautiful sheen, and she had an epiphany. She persuaded her husband to give her a grove of mulberry trees where she studied and domesticated the silkworm; her legacy credits her as well with inventing the silk reel and loom.

In fact, archaeologists have discovered silkworm cocoons in China that were harvested with a knife that date from 4000 BC, and samples of silk textiles used as funeral wrapping have been found that date to 3600 BC. The Chinese held the secret to silk textile production for nearly 3000 years; the royal court even decreed that anyone who shared the method would be put to death.

Silk Road merchants brought samples of the luxurious fabric to the Greek and Roman worlds; Pliny the Elder, a contemporary of Julius Caesar, was the first westerner to correctly identify that the royal thread's source was *Bombyx mori*.

It was not until the third century AD that the secrets were stolen in a Japanese plot that involved smuggling moth eggs and four young Chinese weavers, the latter of whom were forced to divulge the sericulture process.

The origins of the residents of Ban Tao and Xam Tai can be traced back to living in the heart of the region where Chinese sericulture developed, and there is no reason to disbelieve that the residents' silk-raising and cloth-making traditions extend back through a hundred, or even two hundred, generations. The process itself has changed little.

We'll start and end with the egg:

The eggs harvested from a new-born silk moth—whose cocoon was allowed to hatch rather than be processed into thread—are stored in a piece of wrapped blue tarp or in a banana leaf and tucked deep into a cool corner away from light and pests. To begin, the sericulturist will place the eggs onto a bed of what the worms will always have as their sole nourishment: fresh mulberry tree leaves. The mulberry trees that have nourished their crop are planted near the riverbank on the Nam Xam, a ten- to fifteen-minute walk from the heart of Ban Tao. The locals complain that there is a shortage of mulberry trees, and a rare frost in early 2016 eliminated the ability to harvest leaves for several weeks, delaying the anticipated silk schedule and deepening the broad concern about maintaining a sustainable source of hand-reeled silk.

The tiny white worms grow quickly, molting four times, as they nibble the regularly replenished mulberry leaves, and at three to four weeks they have stretched to almost two inches long and are as wide as a pencil, albeit squishier. In one month, silkworms gain 10,000 times their birth weight.

It is now that the worms heed a call from Nature and begin to twirl their heads and spin their thin thread; the sericulturist now attaches the twirling worm to a thin stick of bamboo, which is then pinned onto a mesh board with hundreds of other cocoon makers. For two days, the worms produce "liquid silk" (a protein called fibroin) made in two glands, that they extrude through spinnerets in their heads. This liquid is coated with another protein called sericin, a protective gum, which hardens upon contact with air and which gives raw silk

Eggs newly laid on silkworm cocoons.

a "crunchy" texture that will be softened in the dye process. In those two days, the worm spins about one mile (1600 m) of this dual-protein filament, and it takes about 1500 silkworms, and 110 pounds (50 kg) of mulberry leaves, to produce one pound (0.4 kg) of silk.

Looking at the silk fiber under a microscope reveals filaments five to ten microns wide that have a triangular cross-section with rounded corners. Thus, the flat surfaces of this fiber reflect light only at precise angles to the viewer, giving silk its peculiar, royal shimmer.

The outermost part of the cocoon, which is the portion first woven as the worm encases itself, is the coarsest thread. The innermost strands of the cocoon–those

Left: Silkworm cocoons fully spun and attached to a bamboo frame. Center: Silkworm cocoons being picked and sorted. Right: Silkworm larvae after reeling the silk. The golden larvae will be eaten, the black ones thrown out.

spun at the end of the worm's spinning activity–offer the finest strands.

A dedicated reeler may wish to separate these qualities of thread into three categories: fine, medium, and coarse. Some weavers, or projects, may demand a finer strand of silk, perhaps for its sharpness in a refined textile design. Others may prefer the warmth and fuzziness of the coarser thread for their project. The weaver's effort and skill is no less demanding with any thickness of strand; the work of weaving is the same, but the effect can be different on the completed textile.

Most reelers and weavers in Xam Tai District, however, opt for the efficiency and practicality of not separating the three grades of silk, and creating, in essence, a "medium grade" of silk where thinner and thicker silkworm fibers are meshed together in each single thread of silk. This continuous and consistent fiber meets the needs of nearly every weaving project.

The worm, now undergoing its transformation in the cocoon, will follow one of two pathways forward.

One miraculous path, if the cocoon is left unmolested for twelve to fourteen days, leads to the emergence of a rather plain white moth. The moth exudes a bit of brown spit that dissolves a spot on the inside of the cocoon through which it pulls itself free, eager to share its...uh...heart with an emerging neighbor of the opposite sex. Quite literally, within minutes of hatching, the frantic males and egg-bloated females perform a forthright and vigorous mating right there on the bamboo hatching tray. The moths flit about for a brief hour or two, spent, and then die. The sericulturalist then removes the fertilized eggs from the tray, wraps them in mulberry leaves, and stores them carefully in covered baskets until the month-long cycle begins again. The chickens scrabble over the dead moths.

The second of the two transformational pathways, thanks to a bit of human creativity and chemistry, is processing the cocoons to create the soft sheen and luxurious drape of the world's must coveted fabric: silk. The silkworm, unfortunately, does not survive to "moth-hood" on this pathway.

Our friend Seuk, a reeler in Ban Tao, shows us the silk-reeling process step by step.

CHAPTER TWENTY-FOUR

# Souksakone of Xam Tai

If this book could present only one talent who personifies Xam Tai's creative artistry, dedicated industry, and cultural leadership, Souksakone is that one. She is Xam Tai's pillar of artistic focus and determined passion, and the widely acknowledged leader of the regional traditional silk art. As the leading dye-master, template designer, and textile businessperson in Xam Tai District, she greatly influences both the tone and the standards for the weaving community.

Souksakone is elegant, confident and earthy. She displays a calm exterior and quick smile that hides a whirlwind of creative talent and "get-it-done" energy. She is married to Hamman, a gentle, quiet man who is always busy with construction projects and other town business; he himself, while supportive of Souksakone, stays out of the textile business. They have two grown children in Xam Tai: Khamkong, as handsome, hardworking, and quiet as his father, and Hak, as elegant, hardworking, and focused as her mother. An older son, Xiengthongst, lives in Vientiane.

We met Souksakone the first year Malaithong came with us as our Xam Tai guide as the two of them, along with Phout, had grown up good friends. As travelers, we felt spoiled at having an "inside contact": there is no greater pleasure than being invited into homes to share companionship and experience the ways of locals. As textile enthusiasts, we felt even more spoiled: here was a knowledgeable weaver, dyer and designer, sharing her expertise and company. As businesspeople, we came to realize that we were uniquely and deeply spoiled: Souksakone has her hands on the pulse of the regional silk and textile culture and industry.

Perhaps the most telling statistic is that in 2016 she had 400 weavers working with her colors and patterns, 200 of whom she calls "master weavers," and she is immersed in every step of the pragmatic realities and creative possibilities of her tradition's textile inheritance.

Her home in Xam Tai is base to a myriad of projects. As a matter of fact, her home, for years, has itself been a project-in-action. When we were introduced in 2007, Souksakone, Hamman and their three children lived in a traditional stilted wood-paneled home set behind a wide hard-pack dirt compound. Every year has seen some transformation. The entire stilted home has moved twice. The first time was in 2010 to make way on one side of their lot for the construction of a stately twelve-room cement guesthouse. In 2014 we arrived to find a new thick-walled cement house for her family with a central room for larger gatherings and her projects, including her floor loom. Souksakone joked that the second floor would be added after we completed our purchases. The age-worn stilted home then crouched on an edge of the lot, leaning over the paved compound. In 2016, we discovered that the old stilted home had been moved to another lot near the market, where they are building another multi-story cement dwelling and shop.

Souksakone's family compound is a treat for the curious. Perhaps a half-completed template pattern (khao nyeung) is stretched on her primary loom. Draped and drying on a horizontally-set bamboo pole may be a dazzle of freshly dyed silk skeins; any color is possible, from bright yellow to rich maroon to true black. Sometimes vats of deep colors bubble and froth on small focused fires, bundles of silk bobbing in each richly colored "soup." Visitors drop in regu-

Opposite: Souksakone, dressed for a formal occasion.

paint-chip handed to her.

As a designer, Souksakone has specialized in Xam Tai's most complex iconography, and her reputation dates back to the beginning of the opening of Laos following the American War. In 1994, the Inside Asia Company, in an effort to promote Laos's silk traditions, held its first weaving competition in Vientiane and twenty-four-year-old Souksakone's two entries, among hundreds of entrants, won both first and second place. In 1999 she again won first place. With a rising reputation in dyeing and design, in 1997 Souksakone reached out to other expert weavers to help her weave her patterns. She would provide the dyed silk and the template pattern, and the weavers would then weave the textiles to her specifications. Twenty years later her success has blossomed and, as noted before, she now manages 400 weavers who work with her colors and designs.

When designing motifs and patterns, Souksakone assiduously adheres to the regional Tai Daeng and Lao Loum traditions, but she also has the confidence to create subtle new design forms. She explains to us that while the traditions are important, each generation needs to make an impact on the art. That is why, in 2009, she introduced tapestry-style weaving, a traditional method of the Tai Lue people, into some of her designs.

She admits that the growing market with western tourists has affected design, especially with regard to color variation. She laughs and explains that now she designs textiles using "sii falang"—that is, "colors for westerners." Some of her finest modern creations are now grounded not in traditional red, black, or indigo, but perhaps in turquoise, or an ivy green. Such a textile might look strange or inappropriate to a traditional shaman, but to a western textile enthusiast eager to decorate an entryway, that non-traditional color might make the sale. Souksakone does not hesitate to intrigue and satisfy this deeper-pocketed, developing market.

Souksakone and Phout (introduced in Chapter 18) are lifelong friends and, like many good friends, they seem to counter-balance each other well. Souksakone is calm and direct; Phout is gregarious and bubbly. Indeed, Souksakone seems the "yin"—the methodical logos—to Phout's "yang"—the unfiltered pathos. In essence, these two represent the local textiles not only as two of the gatekeepers of the art and its integration into the twenty-first century, but also as dichotomous tensions that can be found in the art itself, where dedicated order, skilled precision, and real-world pragmatism dance with flamboyant colors, abstruse geometrics, and fantastical mythologies.

Souksakone speaks hesitantly about the future. She is confident of this generation, but the next? There are so many options that can take people away from their home and traditions, and she fears that tomasat (natural) textiles—those that are hand-reeled and naturally dyed—will become too burdensome for future textile artists to pursue. She acknowledges that even her own daughter, a very competent weaver, has many other opportunities in this modern world to pursue. She shakes her head: "Who will lead when I am no longer here?"

Opposite: A recent textile exemplifies Souksakone's palette created to appeal to Western taste. Above: Souksakone, her daughter, and Phout.

The question hangs in the air.

That said, Maren and I have met some strikingly competent young weavers, and we, along with Souksakone and the other leaders of the community, look to Yiim, Ta, Mai Chom (all profiled in this book) and others as the community's future source of cultural continuity and economic steerage.

CHAPTER TWENTY-FIVE

# The Art of Natural Dyeing

Color is action, the verbs of a textile—and silk's embrace of color, as "choreographed" by talented artisans, yields a peculiarly exquisite three-step dance.

The first step is silk's unique ability to reveal a color's depth. Because of its faceted structure, silk's lustrous fiber reflects and glints with resplendence and warmth. Light seems to reach into the threads, gather courage, and burst outwards with confidence. Color blooms out of silk.

Silk's second dance step with color is its eye-catching ability to play off an interwoven or nearby shade. How colors react with and bounce off their neighbors—how they "pop" and "vibrate" in each others' anticipation—elevates each design to a fuller, more radiant life. A red warp with a green weft can resonate an other-worldly shimmer. A soft orange aside a muted purple can reveal a keen flame glowing with its ember.

The third dance step can only be witnessed when you step back from close scrutiny and embrace the full personality of a textile's interacting patterning and palette choice. Here shimmering shapes and color breathe and frolic in multi-dimensional intensity. Various interwoven motifs—ngueak, hong, siho, and more—slither and flap and parade around and through and over. Indeed, the artist's choice of supplemental colors as the patterns are woven is what most reveals each textile's unique relationship with order and chaos, and the seen and unseen.

Silk skeins being checked for depth of hue by Souksakone.

Natural dyes, made from leaves, roots, berries, bark, animals, and other forest items, are said to yield the richest tones. This is not just the bias of those who believe that tradition, knowledge, and a little sweat have a role in shaping perception. In fact, unlike synthetic dyes, dyes derived from natural materials contain trace amounts of other colors, creating subtle depths and complexities in tone. Synthetic dyes do not contain such breadth or depth as the chemists and factories that create them are, in fact, seeking to manufacture a single, precise, predictable hue.

The town of Xam Tai has a unique relationship with natural dyes. That is, many dyers and weavers continue to make and use them. The majority of villages and weavers in Houaphan Province (and Laos) have turned to the ease of either using pre-dyed factory-made thread, or, if the silk or cotton fibers were harvested from scratch, using a quick, sure synthetic dye that comes in a packet, made in China. After all, synthetic dyes, when used according to directions, are consistent, cheap, readily available, generally fade-resistant and colorfast, and come in a generous number of hues.

Natural dyes, on the other hand, are time-consuming. Dye materials must be collected and processed, and the nuanced chemistry requires an experienced hand. If one is weaving for a marketplace where few buyers are concerned about the source of a fabric's dye, the lengthy step of dyeing with natural materials makes little economic sense. More time spent at the loom usually translates to more income, and time spent at the dye pot is not time spent at the loom.

Not that individual dye artists don't exist. Indeed, many local women who make their families' clothing practice the art of dyeing with indigo, the traditional color for daily-wear cotton clothing. But few individual dyers have the time or skill to master the techniques for creating the enormous range of colors often found in Xam Tai's complex cloths. The fact that only small quantities of dyed thread may be needed for some colors also discourages dyers from learning each color's labor-intensive dye process.

This page and opposite: Lac dyeing process.

from the ovaries of the insect to incubating chambers that are formed in a region of the shell left void when the female's body contracts. Soon, the tiny ½mm long larvae, complete with eyes and legs, hatch and swarm the tree in search of new sapling branches.

The crusty stick lac (in Lao, khang) covering the branches looks like a tube of dry tree sap a half inch (1.5 cm) or more in diameter, and it is harvested just before the new larvae swarm. The resin is easily harvested by trimming the red crust off the infected branches. If one looks carefully, tiny larvae can be seen in the dark red resin. The resin stores easily, although the color becomes browner with time.

Making the dye requires delicately balancing the dye liquor's additives. If the concoction gets too much tannin, the red pigment bleaches out, leaving a clear liquid (which, before petro-chemicals, was the natural source of lac-quer and shel-lac). Cheesman notes that the sudden disappearance of color has invited many taboos to form around the creation of this color:

"To prevent evil spirits entering the dye-pot and stealing the colour, spiked vines may be wrapped around the dye-pot, and a piece of spiky bamboo or a knife is placed on the lid. Women cannot dye [lac] while they are menstruating, and strangers might bring bad luck. For this reason, women often dyed lac secretly in the forest at night."

We have not witnessed these traditional behaviors with regards to dyeing, but such beliefs and understandings may still be alive in more remote villages. Or perhaps our hosts do adhere to such traditions, but do not want to share such personal feelings or project themselves as "of the old ways."

Lac can generate an array of red tones. Most are centered around deep crimson, but lac can be manipulated to generate pink, coral, and even brown. Adding a touch of iron, for example, generates an attractive purplish red.

Another natural source for Xam Tai's red palette comes from the heartwood and roots of sappan wood (*Caesalpinia sappan*). Sappan wood may yield, with alum as an additive, a warm vermillion; adding an alkali edges the dye to magenta; adding iron, the dye yields lilac. Add a bit of tin, and one obtains a shockingly bright pink or purple. Souk, Phout, and Lun all work with sappan wood in addition to lac.

Red can also be created from young teak leaves, and this reddish-purple hue is often used to dye monk's robes, and some dyers prefer the brownish reds that can be derived from the bark of the Burmese ebony tree.

### Souksakone's Recipe for Red Dye from Lac

Rinse 1 kilogram (2.2 lb) of stick lac and let sit for a few minutes.

Pulverize the stick lac with a

mortar and pestle.

Remove any sticks as you pulverize.

Soak lac overnight in a large kettle of water, then strain through cheesecloth.

Or alternatively: Soak pulverized lac for 30 minutes in a pot of hot water, strain the lac through cheesecloth. Repeat three times, straining all the dye liquid into a single kettle.

Discard the faded lac solids. (They will be used by another person for their resinous quality. We have seen it used to glue together the bamboo parts of a traditional kaen [mouth-organ] and to glue the hilt of a knife to its blade.)

Boil the dye bath.

Immerse a dozen skeins of silk (each weighing about 50 gm) in the dye bath and soak until the desired color is obtained (30 to 60 minutes).

Souksakone's silk has been pre-treated with alum as described earlier. A common traditional method for pre-mordanting is to first soak the silk for 15 minutes in water that had been boiled with a combination of "sour leaves" from the acidic *Acacia rugata* and tannic *Symplocos racemosa* trees before dipping the skeins into the dye bath.

Yes, the recipe seems simple. However, slight variations generate different outcomes. The dye artist who is seeking certain depths, tones, and shades must consider several factors: the qualities, age, and amount of the stick lac, the type of mordant, the qualities and amount of raw silk, the temperature of the water and the silk's soaking time, the nature of the rinsing, the day's humidity and temperature, and more. These all influence the nature of a dye-lot's "rich red."

Souk watches her dyes attentively. She feels the powdered lac for texture, and carefully assesses its state after it is strained; she stirs the pots carefully, assessing the qualities of the broth and bubbles. A little more of this; a few more minutes of that. There is no timer, and she has four other projects going on, including taking a lead on putting together a delicious lunch.

So let's pause at this moment and regard: Souksakone at the dye pot. Here we find a telling snapshot of present-day Xam Tai's unique and modern spirit. Souksakone, clad in cotton capris and a polyester shirt, engaged in another work day; she wears a mask to avoid breathing the powder of her dyes and additives. She works methodically, simultaneously teaching us and creating dyed skeins for her weavers in front of her street-side home on her recently paved front compound, which doubles as her guesthouse's parking lot. She does not use a thermometer, pH meter, scale, stainless steel pot, or machine-graded powders. Three dyes are simultaneously in process, hence all the pots and fire pits. A pile of recently-delivered bricks destined to form her home's second story lie to one side. Any minute, pretty much guaranteed, there will be a motorcycle delivery,

This page and opposite: Fresh indigo dyeing process.

and, when overlapping a rich red (as it often does), lends a royal attitude to a formal phaa sabai. Souksakone has a plastic garbage can of haem soaking next to her can of kor ben.

### Souksakone's Recipe for Yellow Dye from Haem

Peel and chop the root into thin slices. Fresh or dried haem can be used.

Soak the haem overnight in water.

Boil for 30 minutes, strain through cheesecloth and save the water.

Add more water to the haem; boil and strain again.

Mix the two waters together, and boil one hour.

Add processed silk skeins (for every kilogram "[2.2 lb]" of silk, use 35 liters "[6.5 gal]" of dye-water)

Boil 30 minutes.

Do not rinse.

Hang to dry.

For a less bright yellow, add lye instead of alum.

A bright yellow may also be obtained from true turmeric root (*Curcuma domestica*), the dye of which is easily obtained by boiling and then adding slaked lime (calcium hydroxide). However, like many yellow dyes, this dye tends to be light fugitive. Also, a pale cream can be derived from the bark of the mango tree, and a golden yellow can be coaxed from the heartwood of the jackfruit tree.

And, as mentioned before, there is a local broad-leafed tree from which Souk has recently derived a fast, sharp yellow. But I don't think she's ready to give up that recipe yet.

### · MAKING GREEN ·

Green can often be obtained by overdyeing blue on yellow-dyed threads. For example, silk dyed with indigo to a pale blue can be overdyed with a yellow dye from haem to create a gentle green.

A forest green is derived from the leaves of the bueak (*Marsdenia tinctoria*), a common jungle vine whose leaves contain an indigo pigment. The leaves are dampened with boiling water and crushed with a bit of slaked lime; the resulting juice adheres well to silk. Add lye, and the result is turquoise. Boil the silk in the dye bath for a bit longer, and the turquoise transitions to a steely gray. Of course, every color in between is also available.

In Xam Tai, however, fresh indigo leaves are most often used to make a verdant green. Obtaining this color from Laos's common source of indigo, *Strobilanthes flaccidifolius*, does not require that the leaves be oxygenated in a vat.

### Souksakone's Recipe for Green from Fresh Indigo (Hohm)

Rinse one armload of fresh indigo leaves and stems.

With a mortar and pestle, pound it more than you think—feel free to add more leaves.

Add the pulverized leaves to a liter of water and stir vigorously with your hands.

Submerge the skeins of silk in the chunky paste of leaf and water and stir as vigorously as possible without damaging the skeins.

Rest, and then stir vigorously again.

Repeat, then repeat again.

Lift skeins out of the pot and, with your hands, shake the skeins to remove the solids as best you can.

Set skeins aside.

Squeeze the pulverized leaves, putting the liquid back into the pot and discarding the solids.

Soak the skeins again in the liquid.

Shake off any bits of indigo leaf solids by inserting both hands into the skein and snapping them outward, stretching the skein.

Rinse, and hang to dry.

We wish we could be more precise, but so much of the process seems based on textures, mid-process color-tones, and the shade and qualities of the residue and water that Souksakone is measuring with her years of experience. This process, by the way, left Souksakone's hands a distinct warm green color that she wore for a couple days.

### · MAKING ORANGE ·

Orange is easily obtained from annatto (*Bixa orellana*), a common wild shrub with scores of prickly pods to protect the seeds from which the dye is extracted. Annatto, or achiote, is a common dye world wide, and the package of butter in your refrigerator most likely lists it as a coloring agent.

To extract the dye, annatto seeds are boiled in water and then rubbed vigorously. The resulting liquid is the dye bath for the skeins of silk. Alum may be used as an in-mordant to fix the color. Annatto tends to be light fugitive, however, so it is used sparingly in textiles.

Orange can also be created by overdyeing. Soaking yellow, haem-dyed skeins in a dye bath of lac (not too long!) offers a range of orangey hues.

### · MAKING PURPLE ·

Purples are obtained by blending red and blue dyes, and sappan wood by itself can yield purple tones. Phout also makes an iridescent jewel-tone purple using baby mango tree leaves and water obtained from soaking naturally purple or black grains of glutinous rice.

Virtually every color of the spectrum can be achieved in natural dyes using materials found in the jungles of northeastern Laos, and the regional dyers today not only expertly reproduce colors using the processes that have served previous generations, but also actively explore alternate natural processes and materials to generate new hues and tones.

CHAPTER TWENTY-SIX

# The Art of Silk Weaving: Tools and Techniques

Watching the deft finger work and smooth arm motions of a master weaver is mesmerizing, not unlike the pleasure of watching a virtuoso on the piano. However, unlike the fleeting sounds shaped by a pianist's efforts, the talent of the weaver captures and commits an intricacy of color and form. Indeed, contemplating a master weaver's phaa phi mon, whether it is still on the loom or hanging on our living room wall, has, at least for us textile enthusiasts, the same emotional power and vitality as listening to a great concerto.

A young weaver in Ban Tao works at her loom.

## The Traditional Lao Floor Loom and Plain Weave

The floor loom used in Xam Tai, and for that matter throughout much of Laos, is a simple and clever, and accommodates a myriad weaving techniques. While the design has undergone modest modifications over recent generations, its basic design goes back many centuries. Phout (with Malaithong translating) took the time to show us the steps, one by one, and explain the mechanics of the loom and the weaver for the three most common local weaving styles: plain weave, continuous supplemental weft, and discontinuous supplemental weft. She promised to slowly show us each step as if we had never before seen a working loom.

Phout's floor loom looks like any other Lao weaver's floor loom in the region. The wooden structure commands a space about four feet (1.3 m) wide, seven feet (2.2 m) long, and five feet (1.7 m) tall—about the size of a four-post twin-sized canopy bed. Looms are usually crafted of a non-splintering hardwood, such as teak, and men are almost always the makers of looms and other weaving tools. The framework, which includes a sitting bench, is joined using tongue-and-groove joints so the structure can easily be dismantled and transported or stored. While the wood beams are smoothed to avoid snagging, they are usually left unfinished.

Phout first explained that the loom is made of two primary parts: the frame and the *feum*. The frame consists of the structure's wood beams, which must be strong enough not to bend under tension, the bench that holds the weaver, a few crossbars from which the separate components of the feum are suspended, and four pegged wooden bars, two set above the warp and two below, that will hold each side of the complex-pattern-heddle system's horizontal pattern strings. The frame also has two moving parts: a pair of treadles (foot peddles that control the heddles), and a cloth beam that crosses in front of the weaver's lap and upon which she wraps the newly completed rows of a textile in progress.

The feum—and here Phout smiled, winked, and tapped at her right temple—is the clever part. It contains all the working parts: the "guts"of the loom, including the reed/beater, plain-weave heddles, and the complex-pattern heddle system (*khao nyeung*); each of these parts will be explained as Phout weaves. It is clever because these parts can be removed as a single unit from the frame, tied into a small bundle, taken to any other floor loom in the region, re-attached to that loom's frame, and—voila—the textile's design can be exactly re-created. Just add the warp and weft threads and a weaver's time.

When we had asked Phout to weave the man-woman healing cloths that were no longer readily available, she had gone to her collection of stored feum and selected the specific ones that contained a template for a man-woman design. She then loaned that feum to some of her "best" weavers—best because of the cloth's complexity and our high standards—who then mounted the feum onto their own looms and wove the requested cloths.

Once the feum is assembled, the weaver then warps the loom, laying out the textile's foundational threads of silk, cotton, acrylic, or other fiber. To speed up this process, often friends work together. (Phout's loom was already warped and had a partially-completed textile rolled onto the cloth beam, so she had to describe rather than model the preparation of the warp.)

To warp a loom, skeins of the prepared, dyed thread are first wound onto a warp frame. The overall length of the resulting warp is triple or more the loom's length, perhaps 24 feet (7 m) or more. On a Lao loom, the number of threads wound on this long frame will be double the number of teeth in the loom's reed, since two warp threads will pass through each thin opening in the reed. The number of threads across the warp can range from 30 to 80 per inch, depending on the density chosen for the fabric. A narrow phaa phai shoulder cloth might require only 250 warp threads, whereas the widest, densest phaa phi mon may require 2500 or more threads to generate its width.

A Lao floor loom with khao nyeung patterning device.

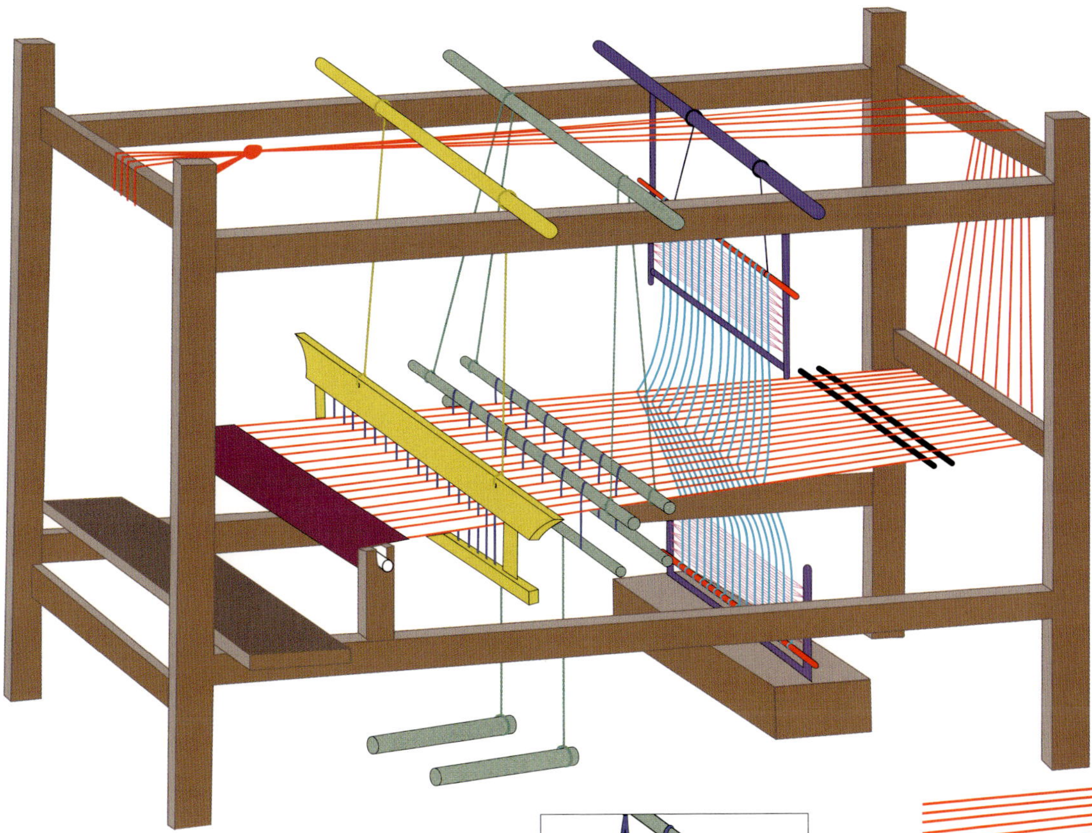

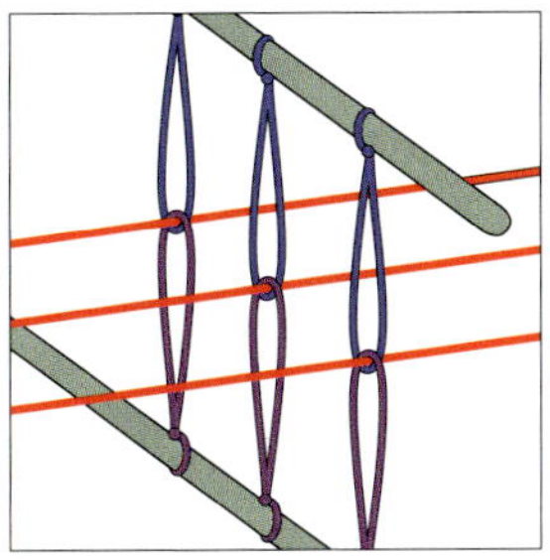

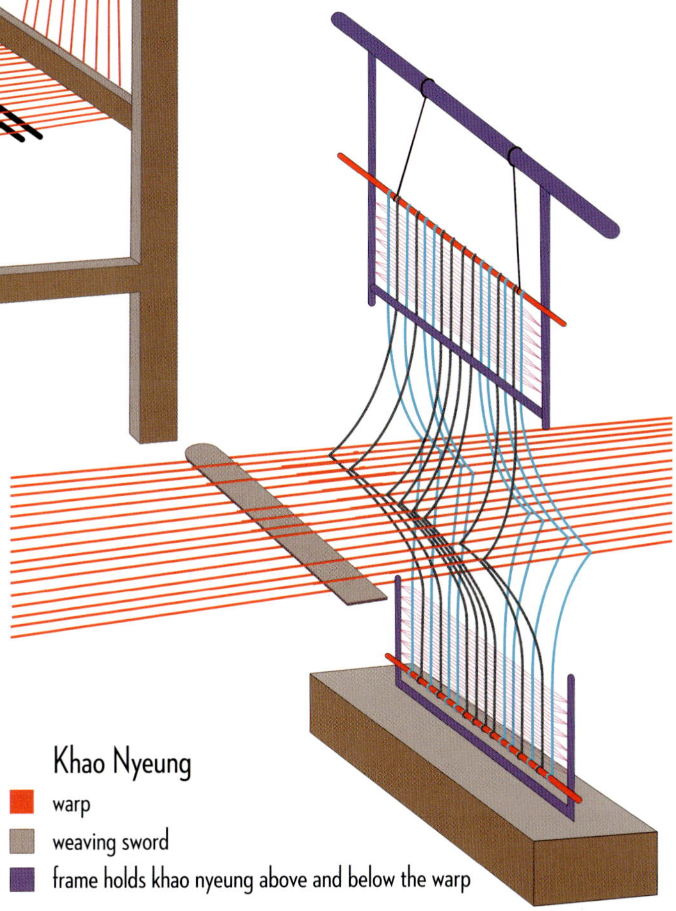

## Full Loom

- loom frame
- reed/beater hung from a suspension rod
- plain weave heddles hung from a suspension rod
- treadles
- frame to hold the khao nyeung
- warp threads
- woven textile wound on cloth beam
- khao nyeung

For a glossary of weaving terms, see next page.

Above: Each plain weave heddle, consists of upper and lower loops, tied to its shed stick. The top and bottom strings loop through each other, creating an eye through which its corresponding warp thread is passed. The heddles on the plain weave shafts are about 6 inches in length. The heddles on the khao nyeung are about 4 feet in combined length.

## Khao Nyeung

- warp
- weaving sword
- frame holds khao nyeung above and below the warp

Above: Khao nyeung open for one row of pattern. The (black) vertical strings are pulled forward and the (blue) strings are pulled back, as separated by the horizontal pattern strings. The (black) strings are to be lifted, raising their respective warp threads, and the sword is to be slid between the resulting shed. The sword will be turned on edge to increase the size of the shed so that the weaver can hand-pick supplemental weft colors for that row.

To assemble the warp onto the loom, each thread must first be passed through its appropriate heddle (explained below) and the narrow teeth of the reed before being tied onto the cloth beam. The reed is the device that separates and holds the warp threads evenly across the loom. On western looms, this is usually called the beater, and the spaces are called dents. The reed's teeth are traditionally made of thin bamboo, and there is a special device to help fit the thread through. A recent addition to the artists' repertoire of tools is the introduction of the steel-toothed reed, which provides a finer gap thanks to steel's strength.

## A SELECTED VOCABULARY OF WEAVING TERMS

**beater:** The loom part that presses newly-woven weft threads against previously woven threads to make a compact textile. On Lao floor looms, the same implement functions as both reed and beater.

**bobbin:** A thin stick upon which prepared thread is wound. The bobbin, stored in the shuttle, unwinds its thread as it passes through the open warp shed.

**cloth beam:** The rotating wooden bar upon which the completed textile is rolled as it is woven. On a Lao loom, the cloth beam is supported directly in front of the seated weaver.

**discontinuous supplemental-weft weaving:** The weaver passes shorter lengths of different-colored weft through the shed in accordance with the pattern dictated by the khao nyeung.

**feum:** In Laos, the elements that comprise the "working guts" of the floor loom: the comb/beater, plain-weave heddles, khao nyeung, and warp leads.

**heddle:** A pair of strings that, when mounted on a loom in series, is used to lift a warp thread. Raising and lowering the heddles creates a shed, or opening, in the warp through which the weft threads are laid.

**khao nyeung:** On a Lao loom, the supplemental complex-pattern heddle system that records the pattern and isolates each weft row's design for the weaver. It is composed of vertical heddle strings and horizontal pattern strings.

**plain weave:** A common, basic fabric structure in which the weft threads alternate over and under each subsequent warp thread.

**reed:** Warp threads are passed through the spaces between its teeth, keeping them parallel and in order. The reed/beater is suspended so that it can swing toward the weaver to pack newly-woven weft picks in place (see "beater").

**selvedge:** The edges of a textile formed when the weft threads turn to go in the opposite direction.

**shaft:** A set of heddles which raises and lowers a selection of warp threads.

**shed:** The space created when some warp threads are lifted and some remain down. For plain weave and continuous supplemental-weft weaving, the shuttle carrying the weft passes through the entire width of this space.

**shuttle:** A wooden bobbin holder, shaped like a canoe, that carries the weft thread(s) through the shed.

**sword:** On a Lao floor loom, a wooden blade that is inserted into the gap between the separated warp threads and that holds open the pattern sheds for discontinuous-weft weaving. The blade is held in place by the tension of the upper and lower warp threads that it separates.

**treadle:** A lever pressed by the foot to raise or lower a shaft.

**warp:** The long threads in a textile that stretch away from the weaver and are held under tension by the loom.

**weft:** The horizontal threads of a textile that go from left to right.

The steel-tooth reed also has a greater heft, and thus takes less arm strength to beat the weft threads into place.

Phout said that weavers now can buy in the marketplace a variety of reed widths complete with two pre-strung sets of heddles (for plain weave), a blank complex-pattern heddle system (khao nyeung), and warp leads of poly-cotton thread slipped between each reed's tooth; a weaver can then tie her own threads to each of the pre-threaded warp leads to pull her own warp thread through the reed's narrow teeth and the heddles, avoiding a tedious process. Of course, if weaving a pattern from a pre-used feum, the previous weaver would have kindly left the ends of her warp threads going through each narrow gap in the reed and heddles to be the leads for the next weaver. The marketplace does not yet supply feum with the complex-pattern heddle system pre-strung with a design.

Once tied onto the cloth beam, the warp threads are then stretched the full length of the loom (going through the reed and heddles), around a wooden bar on the loom's far side, up, and reversing direction, back over the top of the loom over the weaver's head, where it is then tied to the loom's top bar with any excess warp stored in a bag tied to the loom's frame. (There is no warp beam on the Lao loom). The weaver ties a slipknot with the warp threads that are over her head, which will allow her to easily adjust the tension as the textile is woven and rolled onto the cloth beam.

When Phout had warped her loom, she explained that she had also passed each pair of warp threads through a loop, called a heddle, created by two nylon strings that run perpendicular to the warp threads. One of these vertical nylon strings looped downward from a thin bamboo stick placed above the warp strings; the other vertical string looped upward from an identical stick that ran under the warp. Each pair of horizontal warp threads was caught in the center of this set of two vertical nylon string loops; thus, if the vertical pair of strings was pulled upward, the entrapped pair of warp strings would also be raised, and if the vertical strings were pulled downward, the warp strings would follow.

Each heddle-string set is attached, top and bottom, to two thin bamboo sticks that run the width of the warp, and each pair of bamboo sticks holds a selection of heddles; on western looms, this selection is called a shaft. When the shaft is lifted by the weaver using a foot pedal (called a treadle), the set of heddles attached to that shaft lifts as a single unit. Lao floor looms have two basic shafts: one raises and lowers the warp's "even" threads, the other the warp's "odd" threads.

When Phout pushed down with her left foot on the left treadle, one of the two shafts rose up and pulled with it every other heddle, and with them the warp's even threads. A sideways V-shaped gap, called a shed, was thus created between the lifted "evens" and the unlifted "odds." Phout reached into a bowl she had earlier set next to the loom and pulled out a wooden shuttle, a canoe-shaped tool that, in this case, held in its hollowed belly two bobbins of identical silk that would unroll to be the textile's weft threads. Her large, graceful hands cradled the hand-carved shuttle warmly.

With a quick flick of the wrist, she slid the shuttle, right to left, across the surface of the unraised warp threads and through the open shed to her waiting left hand. The bobbins in the shuttle unrolled two threads of silk through the open shed. Phout then closed the shed with a release of the treadle, "trapping" the weft threads under the even and over the odd warp threads. She grabbed the reed on each end with her hands and, with a flip of her wrists, used it as a "beater," pressing the newly-laid weft threads firmly against the previously-woven weft threads.

Phout's current shuttle held two bobbins, so each pass of the shuttle distributed two separate threads. Phout explained that with two threads per reed-tooth in the warp, a double weft would create a firmer textile. Some shuttles are designed to hold up to four bobbins. More weft threads create a thicker cloth, and Phout explained that weavers might choose to use a "four-strand weft" as a feature to lend weight to the textile. Often, the top plain-weave sections of silk sinh are made with a triple-bobbin shuttle to balance to the heavily-brocaded bottom section of the garment.

Phout then said that if she chose to weave a plain cloth with no design threads, she would repeat the process, except this time she would push the right treadle with her foot, lifting the "odd" threads, which would create a new shed; the shuttle would again glide through, left to right this time, and the new pair of weft threads would be beaten into place against the previously set. This process would be repeated over and over. This weaving technique, up to this point, is called plain weave.

### Continuous Supplemental Weft Weaving (*Khit*)

To weave design elements into the warp, the Lao have introduced a clever device called a *khao nyeung*. In English, Boudot and Buckley label the device a "complex-pattern heddle system"; Cheesman refers to the kao nyeung as "long, vertical string pattern shafts."

The khao nyeung provides a unique selection of heddles—essentially, customized shafts—for the weaver, allowing any collection of heddle strings to be selected for any single line of supplemental weft threads. It also "record(s) the full sequence of shed openings for a given motif, so that the weaver's contribution is limited to selection of weft colour and number of wefts" (Boudot and Buckley). In essence, the khao nyeung is the instructions to the weaver, written by a designer, for the textile's precise design. For those familiar with looms, it functions much as a drawloom or Jacquard loom.

The khao nyeung itself is a set of very long, vertically-strung heddles that are crisscrossed with horizontal pattern strings; it extends from the floor to the top of the loom's frame, and it is stretched directly in front of the weaver, just behind the reed and two plain-weave heddles. The length of each vertical heddle string allows the weaver to easily manipulate the complex-pattern heddle system with a simple reach forward.

Phout showed us how, just as with the plain-weave heddles, each of the many pairs of heddles of the khao nyeung loop around a pair of warp threads at its midway point between the floor and the top of the loom frame; if the vertical heddle strings were pulled upward or downward, the single pair of warp threads strung through that heddle would also be pulled upward or downward. A line of supplemental pattern weft is creat-

Mai Chom separates the vertical heddles using the horizontal pattern string.

ed when the weaver lifts a custom grouping of heddles (and hence warp threads) to create a uniquely patterned shed through which the shuttle and bobbin can pass. This customized shed, once closed and with the threads beaten, will reveal a continuous, decorative line of "on again, off again" color as determined by that unique shaft. In row after row of this supplemental weft-thread placement, each unique line of color distribution from each pass of the shuttle will generate the motifs on the textile.

How the weaver selects each specific arrangement of vertical heddle-strings for each custom shed is determined by the horizontal pattern strings that are interwoven through the vertical heddle strings of the khao nyeung. These horizontals have been carefully arranged by a template-maker (in this case, Phout) to cross in front or in back of each paired set of vertical heddle strings. The ends of these horizontal pattern strings are loosely looped onto small wooden pegs set to the left and right of the khao nyeung; each peg holds a dozen or more of these horizontal strings. The khao nyeung on Phout's loom has several hundred horizontal pattern strings: about half stretch across the heddle strings at Phout's seated eye-level, and the other half stretch across below the warp threads at shin level.

To isolate the heddles for each custom shed, Phout reaches forward with her hands, unloops both ends of the lowest horizontal pattern string above the warp, and, arms wide, slides the string down through the network of vertically-aligned heddles to just above the warp threads; she then pulls the horizontal string taut

Mai Chom inserts her sword to open the shed in the warp threads that were separated by the pattern string.

between her hands and pushes her arms forward and back, separating the individual heddles that had been set in front of the horizontal pattern string from the heddles that had been placed behind. This opens up a large triangular gap, or shed, between the separated vertical khao nyeung strings (with the warp threads providing the triangle's base); the apex of the triangle, facing Phout, consists of the selection of heddles that is to be lifted to create a customized pattern weft line.

Holding the detached pattern string in her left hand, Phout reaches under the warp threads with both hands, as if hugging the warp, and stretches the string through the triangular opening that mirrors the khao nyeung's opening above the warp; she then reattaches that pattern string to two pegs, one on the right and one on the left, that were set under the warp threads (mirroring the pegs above). This saves that string's unique pattern for future use.

Sitting back upright, Phout grasps with her left hand all the forward heddle strings and manually lifts them, which lifts the attached warp threads to create the custom shed in the warp. To hold that shed open, Phout, with her other hand, slides in a smooth piece of teakwood three inches (8 cm) wide and a quarter inch (1 cm) thick, the length of which was a little wider than the width of the warp. In English, this tool is called a sword. Placing the sword on edge inside the shed, where it is held tightly by the tension of the upper and lower warp threads, gives Phout the space for a second shuttle to slide through—this one also with a double bobbin—which deposits two lines of red weft thread patterning.

After the weft threads are laid in, Phout removes the sword, beats the newly-laid threads against their predecessors, and then, the entire process starts over: weave a row of plain weave using the two-heddle system, then weave the threads of supplemental color through a customized shed using the pattern pre-determined by the khao nyeung.

When all the horizontal pattern strings she had wanted to use above the loom have been used and are now set under the loom in saved order, Phout explains that the weaver would then reverse the direction of the process, using the top stored pattern string that is now under the warp as the next active pattern string, and then the one under that. Thus, each pattern string stored under the warp is used again, one by one, and returned to the top. This process of "weaving a pattern down and then back up" explains why most Lao textiles display figures woven in mirror image. As such, a supplemental diamond shape can be woven "down" by using a set of pattern strings that creates a triangle, and then these same "memory strings" can be reused in reverse order, bottom to top, generating an inverse triangle, which thus creates a full diamond.

The horizontal pattern strings of the khao nyeung are a fairly recent adaptation. Older textiles were woven using khao nyeung that had lengths of thin bamboo, called "memory sticks," instead of string. However, increasingly complex design work makes the use of bamboo sticks difficult. Some patterns, particularly some of the most dynamic modern silks, require a thousand lines of horizontal template pattern; such a bundle of sticks would be too unwieldy to either manipulate at the loom or store in the feum.

Modern khao nyeung, like those Phout, Souksakone, Lun, and Chola create, are made with thin nylon string, as nylon doesn't rot or fray, takes a great force to break, and requires little storage space. That said, we still do see memory sticks being used, usually by elders or novices, who are working with simpler design patterns.

Phout took a private couple minutes with her loom to "unweave" the single line of supplemental color she had just woven during the demonstration. While she had wanted to show us continuous supplemental weft, where each supplemental horizontal thread goes from selvedge to selvedge (one edge of the textile to the other edge), the truth was that the textile set on her loom actually required discontinuous, not continuous, supplements.

I had thought the recent line of weft on Phout's textile looked out of sync with the previously woven section. But it can be hard to tell—especially because the weaver is looking at the backside of the textile as it is being woven. Many weavers have a rearview mirror scavenged from a motorcycle sitting beside the loom, and occasionally check the patterning on the underside to make sure that the emerging motifs are precise. Phout said that it takes some experience to "see" the front of a textile when looking at its back, but after forty years of practice, she conceded, she has developed a knack for it.

Phout threw out a quick loud sentence when she finally had pulled out the sample thread and laughed. Malaithong also laughed, and so Maren and I did too, but the line was left untranslated. Perhaps Phout had said "I hate it when I have to pull out a thread," or perhaps "This reminds me of teaching my daughter." Or perhaps, "The nutty things I will do for these falang." It really didn't matter; it was still funny.

### Discontinuous Supplemental Weft Weaving (*Chok*)

When a weaver does not want a supplemental pattern thread to run the full width of the textile, she must hand-pick a selection of supplementary pattern wefts rather than using a shuttle and bobbin. This discontinuous-weft method places lines of color on a textile, be it a single dot that is to be the eye of a serpent, or a 6-inch (20 cm) line that shapes the back of an elephant.

Xam Tai's most refined and intricate textiles—the ceremonial phaa sabai, phaa phi mon and phaa biang—are woven using the discontinuous supplemental weft technique, as are the most opulent sinh.

Phout, having pulled the single line of continuous thread out of the weft, now returned to the moment where she had opened up her khao nyeung and again opened up the shed for the unique pattern line and stuck in her wooden sword. However, instead of sliding her shuttle and bobbin of supplemental color through the shed, she reached up to the loom's beam above her head and to her right where she had hung eight small batches of differently-dyed silk threads. The palette for this textile included shades of yellow, blue, red, and orange.

Phout pulled out a small amount of the yellow silk—perhaps four strands each two feet (.6 m) long. In one deft move, she slid the strands under several of the raised warp threads on the farthest left side of the custom shed, fingered a quick knot, and fed the yellow through a section of the pattern's shed—perhaps two inches (5 cm)

A plain-weave weft follows a row of discontinuous supplementary pattern wefts.

of yellow had been placed in the textile. She reached up and pinched a bit of red thread and knotted it on the warp threads next to where she had tied off the yellow. A quick play of her fingers on the raised warp threads again and a bit of red had been placed as a supplemental line of weft in the emerging textile. In this manner, Phout's fingers danced cross the entire line of weft, tying on a variety of supplemental colors under a selected section of the lifted set of warp strings.

These supplemental threads are usually of several strands to create a heftier, brocade-like pattern, and different effects can be created using thicker or thinner lines of hand-picked colors. More threads lend a softer, fuzzier appeal, while fewer supplemental threads speak to exactitude and cooler precision, and let the ground colors show through a bit more.

The benefit of facing the back of the textile while it is being woven is revealed in this process as well: it allows the weaver to knot each new discontinuous pattern thread on the silk's backside, leaving the tidy, smooth texture and crisp motif outlines one expects from a fine textile on the front.

There was more supplemental thread than that one line needed, and Phout smoothed the extra length of colored thread toward herself over the completed portion of the textile. On subsequent lines

A weaver in Saleui uses supplementary pattern warp stripes in her indigo-dyed sinh.

of supplemental weft, she would use that extra length rather than reach for new weft threads.

The weaver herself, and not the designer, very often selects the specific reedination and placement of supplemental colors that shape and accentuate (or disguise) a textile's motifs and other pattern traits. This aesthetic overlap of design and color—"color-play—offers insight into a master weaver's clever mind, talented fingers, and aesthetic virtuosity.

At the end of each row of discontinuous supplemental weft, Phout closed the custom shed, beat the threads firmly into place, and then repeated the full process:

• lift one shaft of plain-weave heddles with one foot treadle;

• lay a two-bobbin line of thread by sliding a shuttle through the shed created by the shaft;

• beat the newly laid ground threads against the forming textile using the reed;

• isolate a unique set of heddles (and thus warp threads) using the horizontal pattern strings of the khao nyeung;

• replace the just-used horizontal pattern string on the alternate side of the warp threads;

• lift the now-isolated, forward heddle strings and slide in the sword to hold the pattern shed open;

• hand-pick a row of supplemental silk threads;

• remove the sword and beat the supplemental colored silk threads against the forming textile;

• use the other treadle to lift the other plain-weave shaft;

• 1repeat processes 2–9

Phout wove a few more lines of textile silently. Stepping behind her, I enjoyed watching the smooth, gentle sway of her arms and upper body, and then a centered moment of focused intent as the supplemental colors were picked at even pace from left to right. She made it look easy—a virtuoso on her instrument.

Afterwards, Phout proudly showed us a selection of patterns that were her designs and stored in her home. Each was tied in it own tidy, transportable feum. Some of these feum, she said, were recreated from old, inherited patterns, allowing the designs of elders and ancestors to be re-created and remain vivid and present. Others were of her own design that she had created over her forty years of working with the loom.

## Supplemental Warp Weaving (*Muk*)

Another regional textile style requires that the loom provide a supplemental warp in addition to the plain-weave warp, which allows the weaver to create patterning in the warp threads in addition to the discontinuous horizontal patterns in the weft. This technique is used primarily in the weaving of traditional sinh. Mai of Xam Tai, whom we visited in on page 66, is weaving a cotton sinh on a loom that uses a supplemental warp system.

In this technique, a second set of warp threads extends from the cloth beam, through the reed's teeth (just like the primary warp), through its own supplemental warp heddles (but not the plain-weave heddles), and then angles downward and wraps around a bottom beam on the far side of the loom, where it turns the corner and goes upward, eventually paralleling the primary warp threads across the top of the loom frame. Both warps are knotted, separately, above the weaver's head. The tension on the two warps must be identical to prevent sagging, and in this technique a weaver has to exercise extra patience to monitor and constantly adjust these dual sources of tension.

These supplemental warp threads are kept below the regular warp threads until they are "drawn into" the main warp using a set of separate supplemental shafts that only lift a selection of these supplemental warp threads. The warp thread shafts are not a part of the khao nyeung, but an entirely separate shaft system similar from the two plain-weave shafts used for the primary warp.

In Lao weaving, supplemental warp threads are usually white and are usually designed to weave thin patterned stripes that are about an inch apart and run the length of the textile. This pattern offers an elegant touch on the dark plain-weave background on a sinh, and can also lend further complexity to a piece being additionally woven with discontinuous supplemental weft threads.

## Tapestry-Style Weaving (*Yiap Koh*)

Although relatively new to the Lao Loum and Tai Daeng weavers of Xam Tai, tapestry weave is not new to the region. The Tai Lue people of northern Vietnam and northwest Laos have traditionally used the tapestry technique to weave portions of their skirts, and it is thought that the Tai Neua people of Houaphan Province "borrowed" it from them. The Phuan people in northwest Laos also have woven using the tapestry technique for at least 150 years.

Souksakone first introduced the tapestry weave into Xam Tai's textiles in 2009, and since then Phout and other weavers (including sixteen-year-old Ta of Meung

Kuan on page 106) have designed and woven "tapestry weave" panels into some of their textiles. Currently, the tapestry-woven panel is limited to adorning traditional healing clothes (phaa sabai), whose center panels were traditionally left as plain weave. In a design by Souksakone or Phout (or the prodigy, Ta), this element tends to be unusually complex, and requires the skills of a master weaver. Tapestry weave is particularly challenging to do well, as it requires incredibly precise attention to weft tension.

Above: Handspun cotton skeins are tied in a precise pattern in preparation for dyeing. Right: Bobbins holding dyed wefts are tied on a string to maintain the correct order for weaving.

Because the technique is demonstrated in a phaa sabai's center panel—roughly, its middle third—a weaver must initially weave the first third of the cloth using the traditional discontinuous supplemental weft method. When the weaver reaches the center panel, she puts away her bobbin and shuttle, as this tapestry-woven panel will not include plain-weave weft threads. The khao nyeung can now be ignored as well.

Instead, the weaver proceeds to create each weft by linking portions of differently colored threads around each other in a single lock around the warp thread where the weft threads meet. The series of interlocked threads for each line of weft must maintain perfect tension for the emerging motifs to be even and centered as they are shaped, line by line. The weaver's talent is evident not only in the pattern created (which is not stored in a template, but rather "kept in the weaver's mind") but also in the precision of links across the textile and her ability to keep the horizontal tension of each color in each row consistent as the hundreds of rows of threads are assembled.

Tapestry weave can generate bold, blocky designs, and our American audience often comments on how this portion of the textile reminds them of Navajo rug designs. The style does offer a dramatic shift in design from the intricate complexity of discontinuous supplemental-weft geometric motifs usually evident on ceremonial textiles. Whether this technique will endure as it is being now practiced remains to be seen. Ultimately, the market will determine whether the technique is seen as an enhancement of, or a distraction from, the traditional silk art of Xam Tai.

## Weft Ikat Weaving (*Matmi*)

Ikat-style weaving (in Lao, *matmi*) is common in Houaphan Province, although we don't see much of it in Xam Tai District. However, villages like Saleui and Na Sala, which are located an hour west of Xam Neua, are renowned for their quality matmi sinh. Matmi is less a weaving technique and more a different preparation and dyeing process that yields a strikingly different effect. In matmi, the threads of the weft are dyed before the weft and warp threads are woven together; when the threads are finally assembled using plain weave, the pattern then emerges on the textile.

A dyer who is preparing thread for matmi begins by spinning cotton (or sometimes, reeling silk) and then wrapping the threads around two sides of a wooden rectangular frame about 2 feet (0.6 m) tall and 2.5 feet (0.75 m) wide.

To wrap a sinh's worth or more of weft thread onto the frame, and weaver rotates the entire frame on a hand-built implement. As the frame rotates, the weaver directs the threads being wound into notches that have been cut into the frame every inch (2 cm) or so.

The width of the wooden frame is precisely the width of the loom's warp on which it will be woven so the selvedges (the edges of the textile) will end up being exact and even. Once the wound threads are wrapped onto the frame, the weaver ties off sections of the thread in a chosen pattern, wrapping these portions tightly with plastic wrap (before plastic, fiber derived from the trunk of banana trees was used). When the tied threads are dipped into the dye bath (very often indigo), the portion that has been "tied off" in plastic is protected from the dye. After dipping, the weaver waits for the dyed threads to dry, then removes the plastic wrap, revealing the pattern.

Some weavers choose to re-dip a single

Above: A matmi sinh with a naak and flower motif, is stretched on the loom. Top right: Plastic tied on cotton weft for a matmi pattern. Bottom right: Multiple colors are painted on the weft threads with dye and then tied with plastic prior to the full dye bath."

pattern many times into the indigo dye bath to generate a deep rich blue-black; others may prefer a lighter blue, or a reedination of shades of blue as differing sections of the tied-off threads are dipped more often than others. If a more complex coloration is desired, the dyed threads may be tied off into a second pattern (and then a third), and re-dipped into a new dye bath of a different color. The possibilities of creative design are as rich as the dye-baths themselves!

After dyeing, the weaver removes the multi-colored threads from the frame and rewinds these threads onto bobbins; these bobbins must be kept in careful order so the dyed pattern, when these threads are woven into the weft, will re-create the planned pattern. After tying the warp threads onto the loom, the weaver finally picks up her shuttle and orderly bobbins of pre-dyed thread and proceeds to plain-weave the multi-toned weft thread. The pattern re-emerges as the weft threads are precisely laid down, one by one, re-creating the pattern that was on the matmi frame, but now with warp threads interwoven to hold it together.

If done with accuracy, the emerging re-created pattern is distinct and sharp. Selvedges must be meticulously maintained, and a broken thread must be precisely re-tied in order to maintain the accurate re-emergence of the dyed pattern. Every throw of the shuttle must distribute the thread precisely. If done sloppily, the threads' two colors may not line up well upon reconstruction leaving a "fuzzy" indeterminate appearance.

Cheesman notes that the region does have a history of weavers using a warp ikat (*matkaan*), a traditional skill of the Tai Neua and Phuan ethnic groups. However, Maren and I have not been privileged see this in action, or even ogle a sample textile.

pattern. Designs for the marketplace should always be fresh." Her sense of balance between the "traditional" and "what is new" marks her as one of the leading artists and entrepreneurs of the region.

Souksakone's mind is always working with patterns as well. In her front room sits a full floor loom, and on its cloth beam we can often find a small section of design woven in less expensive chemically-dyed thread. This would be the first "drawing" of a new design element, a portion of a pattern we might see in next year's creative output.

Souksakone comments that she likes to add a "little change" each year, and she notes that the "old people" like to keep the same patterns while the young like something that is more unique and per-

Left: Khao nyeung for a sinh. Note the pattern concentrated on the right side for creating the sinh border. Below: Close-up of the khao nyeung reveals the pattern to be woven.

haps pushes the boundaries. Her ability to read the market and steer the effort of 400 weavers, each of whom relies on her design and marketing expertise, is essential to local economics.

Both Phout and Souksakone note that the accelerating pace of the era has its effects:

The biggest recent advent? The smart phone and its camera, which Phout tells us has changed how she can communicate instantly with her weavers regarding design and color. A picture can be worth a lot of words.

The toughest modern scourge? Lao weavers from outside of Xam Tai who steal their unique patterns, copying templates without permission, which they then weave to sell for themselves in the competitive marketplace. In Laos, there is no way to trademark or legally "own" a design. Trust and loyalty at the local level usually prevent such theft. But once a design enters the larger urban marketplace, unique designs can be, and are, readily stolen.

As for the many hundreds of dedicated weavers in Xam Tai and Meung Kuan Districts—and you see their faces in the photographs—they range from ages seven to ninety. Some weave part-time, a few hours scheduled around the myriad other responsibilities; others weave many hours every day. Some weave solely to make clothes for their family; some weave to maximize income. School and homework is prioritized for those sixteen and under, allowing the most ardent young weavers perhaps two or three hours a day to create at the loom.

Many weavers, acting as "sole proprietors," weave textile patterns passed down from their elders or of their own creation. Some of these weavers raise, reel, and dye their own silk; others purchase it by the skein in the market, or from a neighbor. Both natural and chemical dyes are available, as are skeins of pre-dyed silk; colorful silk-like acrylic is readily available in the market as well. Many who weave for the tourist market will have a contact—usually a family member—in an urban center who can either sell the textiles directly or consign or sell at wholesale to a shop. As a profession, a "full-time weaver" (perhaps forty hours per week) earns about the same as a government or office worker.

Many expert weavers who earn a "full-time" income, however, are asked—essentially, contracted—to create a textile by another person. This manager will bear the responsibility for:

- choosing and providing the design in a khao nyeung to the weaver,
- supplying the dyed silk to the weaver for that textile,
- paying the weaver directly for her loom-time upon the textile's completion, and
- managing the risk and responsibility for getting it to the marketplace.

Because of this economic arrangement with a manager, many successful silk weavers need to give little thought to the creation of the khao nyeung, as this is provided by the person who holds ultimate responsibility for making sure the textile meets its bottom line—that is, it sells. Which makes sense; the reality is that few rural weavers would be aware of the modern marketplace's trends and expectations, and thus they rely on this manager to determine what makes best practical use of their time at the loom.

At first blush, the craft of the actual weaver herself may seem diminished if she is not responsible for the pattern and seems to just follow the instructions as established in a template-maker's khao nyeung. But the weaver has plenty else to concentrate on beyond working the mechanics of the pattern strings of the template.

The most critical element for the weaver is the requirement of consistency. In the plain weave component of the task, loom tension in both warp and weft must be meticulously adjusted and maintained, and the silk threads must be "beaten" into each other with equal and consistent pressure, row after row. Inconsistencies in the silk thread itself, such as slubs or dye-lot changes, must be dealt with.

While some weavers create all their own colors of silk for a textile (and perhaps raise their own silk as well), the many weavers who work with a manager are supplied with the various colors of needed silk for each textile. As mentioned earlier, this is one reason it makes sense for the dyers to also maintain the role of the manager. In this relationship, the dyer chooses the ground colors—the primary background color(s)—by virtue of the fact that the bulk of the provided silk will need that one color. The manager also provides an array of supplemental colors that she has chosen for the palette of that textile. Some managers may have, as a part of the instructions to the weaver, a very explicit plan for the use of the supplemental colors; other managers will let the weaver, especially if she is more experienced, take responsibility for effectively choosing the colors of the supplemental pattern wefts.

So while the weaver may not have to be concerned with the shape of the motif, how that shape is seen in the completed textile relies on a weaver's visual talent. To make

A weaver displays the first textile she made completely herself from worm to weaving.

a siho stand out, proud and sure, a weaver may wish to color it in white against a red backdrop. A siho's belly often has a series of stripes, and the weaver may choose to have the stripes go from darker to lighter shades, giving the motif greater "lift." Or perhaps the weaver will choose that the stripes remain dark and heavy, adding weight to the figure. Perhaps a bright splash of green for an eye, or perhaps it remains white.

We often can compare identically-patterned textiles, woven with the same khao nyeung, that look dramatically, conceptually different by virtue of how the weaver has chosen, to manage the play of color within the parameters of the design. What jumps out boldly and what hides in subtlety—all this is affected by supplemental color choices (witness the effect of color variation with identical patterning displayed on Phout's man-woman healing cloth on page 112).

The reliance many weavers maintain with a central manager has several benefits:

First, weavers may, if they choose, continue to live a traditional-style life in even the most remote villages; their participation in the cash economy is not dependent on where they weave or with whom they live. A weaver need only get her completed textile to that manager to gain her compensation.

Second, by virtue of being able to remain doing a traditional task in a traditional village, the transmission of cultural knowledge and ethnic heritage remains centered in the family's home and the traditional village setting. Cultural identity remains intact, and the emerging adult generation is not compelled to seek a meager living in an urban sweatshop, as is found in many other developing nations. Thus, children grow up surrounded by their extended families and cultural traditions. Such continuity must contribute to one's inner sense of well-being.

Third, weavers do not need to understand or participate in the business complexities and dynamic economics of the western-style marketplace. Nor does the weaver hold responsibility for measuring the changes in what the market desires from year to year. The expert weaver can focus solely on the weaving task, assured that a member of her own community will provide fair compensation and support.

Fourth, that manager, by virtue of her expertise with the marketplace, can educate the weavers about meeting the unique demands of the current market. For example, if a weaver has a slight imbalance in selvedge tension (where one edge of the warp is tighter than the other), the result is what we call a "banana"—a textile that, when hung, curves noticeably to the left or right. Such a flaw may not be significant if the textile is worn as a shawl. However, western audiences often hang these textiles as wall art, and "bananas" just don't hang or sell well.

Or another problem modern weavers have to address: changing dye lots in a single creation, and using two ever-so-slightly different shades of a vital color. A slight shift in a cloth's ground color from a dark raspberry toward a muted maroon may seem trivial, but such inconsistencies, when hanging in an elegant gallery, are magnified as errors in the western aesthetic. The manager maintains the role of learning about and disseminating this information for the benefit of all. (Oh, the number of beautiful textiles Maren and I have had to reject due to these inconsistencies in weaving and color.)

Finally, the participants in the silk textile economy who work with a manager operate in a cooperative, rather than competitive, environment (reminiscent of the muang of the region's old political order). Every

Souksakone's "drawings" of new design elements.

The naturally-dyed colors pop on this curled-tailed naak textile dyed and designed by Lun.

part of the creative process—from raising the worm to reeling to dyeing to weaving to selling—maintains an essential role, and having a central coordinator assures that all aspects of getting a textile from worm to market runs efficiently. The economic model thus reinforces overall "well-being" by acknowledging the reliance and support between the creative participants, and by providing a more unified voice of leadership both within the community and to the outside world.

Maren and I have deliberately steered clear of inquiring too deeply about the nature of each of their personal and business relationships among the local weavers, dyers, and others. While curious, we are businesspeople and not academics, and we do not wish to invade the corners of our Xam Tai friends' personal or professional lives. As such, we do not ask who is weaving for whom and for how much, and any transaction between locals we witness is left untranslated. We have no doubt, however, that the personal and business politics in such a small and long-isolated community must be a tangle worthy of an ethnographic study, and perhaps a soap opera as well.

Still, despite the visible and hidden realities of local economics and politics, we cannot diminish the romance of seeing so many active floor looms in the shade of so many homes in Xam Tai and Meung Kuan Districts. The gentle click and clack of the shuttle, the thump of the beater, and the intense moment of silence as the supplemental wefts are laid into the warp is a gentle music that speaks to the generations of effort, promise, cooperation, and independence of this healthy and determined community.

CHAPTER TWENTY-EIGHT

# Chola of Xam Tai

Maren, Ari, Zall, and I stumble out of Xam Tai's old low-ceilinged marketplace in the center of town, and the close tropical sun bites sharply into our pale skin as we walk up the paved street. This part of Xam Tai, which is near Souksakone's, has been almost entirely constructed in the last twenty years, and the homes, rather than wooden and on stilts, are made of concrete and squat on the ground, western-style.

To our right, we hear the familiar clicking of a loom, and we peer around a tidy fence to see a young woman at a floor loom on a shaded patio. Ari and Zall (and I admit myself as well) try to pry Maren away from the vision of yet another weaver; we are eager to retreat to the guesthouse for a glass of anything cool and a mid-day break next to the fan. But just try to distract Maren when the shuttle is making time.

"Sabaidee-ee," Maren intones from the gate. The young women—a girl actually—jumps a bit and looks up at the tall blond stranger. She glances to her home, and then back at Maren.

"Sabaidee," she whispers, even though we are ten steps away.

Maren doesn't wait for an invitation, but walks down the slope and up to the loom to examine the narrow white scarf warp she has stretched on the loom. It is not a phaa phai (temple cloth), but rather a unique shoulder scarf of all white with a small bit of bright design, about the size of a coin, every few inches.

"*Ngam lai*," Very beautiful. Maren says. The girl looks down at the ground and sucks in her lips, biting on a nervous smile. Is that a blush?

"*Jaak pii*?" How old are you? Maren asks without looking up from the textile. Maren's fingers rub an edge of the smooth silk.

The girl again looks toward her home, then at us three guys still at the gate, and then back to Maren. "*Sip saung*," she mouths. Twelve. Her eyes again glance up quickly at the three of us at the gate, then Maren, then back to the ground.

Maren continues her close-up examination, and she then, using hand-motions, convinces the girl to unroll the silk from the cloth beam a bit so the textile could be turned over and its front pattern revealed. Each bit of color design appears to be a mayfly, or perhaps a stylized crane fly.

I can see Maren's curiosity spinning, and I know she had a number of questions. By now Ari, Zall, and I have welcomed ourselves to the patio and join Maren beside the loom. Maren points to the figure and, looking the girl in the eye, raises her eyebrows in what we would think would be an inquiring look. The girl stared blankly at Maren, like she is waiting for more. Her large eyes shoot to Ari, then Zall, then me, then back to Maren. She raises her own eyebrows and shrugs.

Maren then starts flapping her arms limply and dances a semicircle. Is she a bird? A bumblebee? There is a second of silence as Maren flaps. Her dance is awfully…uh…jouncy.

The girl bites her lip and stares blankly at Maren's vigorous efforts. Then she snorts—and her hands slap to her mouth to hide the flash of a smile. She swallows a quick laugh, but then Zall lets out a chortle, which in turn gets Ari going.

Maren stops, mid-flap and mid-jounce, and turns toward the group's laugh. "Wha-at?" she asks with mock indignation, and then she joins in the laughter.

Chola at her loom.

Step by step, Chola is "unweaving" an old textile and simultaneously creating a new khao nyeung to re-create the old design.

We are all spared further embarrassment when a woman—the girl's mother, it turns out—comes out from the side door to her home and rescues the girl from both a strange Scandinavian dance and further interrogation.

"Sabaidee-ee", says the woman cheerfully, and we all return her greeting with a quick pressing of the hands under the chin and say "Sabaidee." She grins broadly and nods at the smiling group. She says a few quick words to the girl, who jumps up and dashes into the house. The mom motions with her arms that we should come inside and indeed, the air inside the home is cooler. The girl comes in a minute later carrying a tray with five drinking glasses, a plastic pitcher of water, and a bunch of local bananas—the small fat ones that are so amazingly sweet!

Without Malaithong or another translator, we chat about what we can with our Lao vocabulary of a few dozen words. We learn the girl's name is Paivan, and that mom's name is Chola, and that the family also has an older son who is not at home. We smile, nod a lot, eat bananas and drink the refreshing water. We all laugh at our lack of words, but we all feel together in that loss. Maren communicates that we will return later that day, with Malaithong in tow.

Later that afternoon, we share tea, bananas, apples, and a package of Oreo-like cookies that Chola has purchased, I'm sure, solely for our visit. Chola keeps pushing the platter of food toward the boys, and the more they eat, the wider she smiles. Paivan sits beside her mom, attentive and silent. Chola's husband, Nau Tong, dashes in between errands, eagerly shakes our hands, rummages through a closet, and then disappears out the back door.

With Malaithong's help, we learn that the design Paivan is weaving is a butterfly motif, and that the specific design is unique to the family. The wings are partly folded, hence the more bug-like appearance (so Maren's flapping dance wasn't far off after all). Paivan has been weaving since age seven, and has learned from Chola. Chola herself had begun weaving as a child and had been taught by her mother as well.

We end up purchasing six of Paivan's scarves—all identical save the supplemental colors of the butterfly. Chola also has two large sacks full of other textiles—one of new sinh that had recently been woven by "her weavers," and the other had some handwoven silk and cotton blankets woven in a previous generation. Needless to say, it takes us over an hour to see her textile selection, and we leave with several unique pieces.

Like Lun, Phout, and Souksakone, Chola, now fifty years old, has a fleet of weavers who work with her; in 2016, thirty weavers work under her direction. Chola, however, focuses exclusively on designing and weaving sinh that sell well in the urban markets to Lao shoppers, as opposed to Lun, Phout, and Souksakone who are more focused on ceremonial-style scarves and shawls that seek an international audience of textile enthusiasts.

Almost all of her Chola's sinh are woven using a factory-made poly-cotton warp and weft, which is then decorated with silk supplemental wefts. The silk supplemental threads are raised locally and are a mix of natural and chemical dyes. Her audience, the rising Lao middle class, is less concerned with the ethic of a textile being tomasat, all-natural. Both the poly-cotton ground threads and the absence of natural dyeing hold the textile's cost down considerably (although it is still time-consuming to weave), allowing her to remain more competitive in the marketplace she serves. Her husband delivers textiles in his pickup truck several times a year to their contacts in Vientiane, Luang Prabang, and the southern city of Pakse.

When we visit in 2016, we drop by Chola's home and find her working at her floor loom on the patio.

"Come look at this," Maren says excitedly, her nose about a pencil-length away from Chola's khao nyeung. "Chola is…uh… un-weaving!"

Indeed, Chola is moving the threads of an old textile one by one out of the original fabric and into a newly-forming khao nyeung. An elder's weaving effort is being reborn.

Chola has a portion of a sinh with an attached tiin sinh about four inches (10 cm) wide pinned onto her loom on the backside of her comb. The pattern is very intricate: a writhing set of ngueak in primary colors that had once been somebody's prize sinh. Chola explained through Malaithong that this pattern was uniquely intricate and the ngueak had a particularly delicate and complex interwoven nature.

To "unweave" the pattern and transfer it to her template, Chola first had stripped away several inches of the original sinh's weft threads to free the original warp thread; she then had tied each of the old warp threads to a vertical string of the loom's khao nyeung. Using a flattened wooden blade, Chola then carefully isolated and separated every supplemental weft thread of the old textile that creates the ngueak motif. In essence, she was "unbeating" and "un-handpicking" the threads. Once the row of supplemental weft thread had been pulled away from the rest of the weft, Chola gently inserted a sword on the horizontal plane over and under each warp thread in the pattern that had been established by the original supplemental weft threads. The sword was then turned on edge, separating the warp threads picked out by the discontinuous wefts. The warp threads' corresponding vertical pattern strings were then separated and pulled forward from those not attached to the lifted warp threads. Finally, Chola placed a new nylon horizontal pattern string into the void between the separated sections of the vertical pattern strings, hooking it onto the holding pegs. A new row of design was thus transferred from the old textile into a horizontal pattern string of the forming khao nyeung.

Patiently, Chola will separate the several hundred threads one by one, and the old sinh's pattern would be both preserved and able to be readily replicated.

After explaining this current project, Chola invites us into the cool of her home. Unlike most sparsely decorated Lao homes, Chola and Nau Tong's front room now has a large L-shaped leather-colored couch fronted by a coffee table. On the wall, proudly displayed, are several family photos. Both sets of Chola and Nau Tong's parents, clad in traditional formal wear, look sternly out from formal photos set near ceiling height. The photos of their kids show toothy smiles and western-style clothing.

We again share glasses of water and fresh fruit, and catch up on our families. Paivan, now eighteen years old, lives in Vientiane and studies accounting at the university. No, she really doesn't have time to weave right now, laughs Chola, but perhaps she will find evening time for such in her future. Chola continues to beam with pride as she explains that her older child, her twenty-four-year-old son, is just completing law school in Hanoi, Vietnam. She nods as we update her on our kids in college, and, like many middle-aged parents, we commiserate about high tuition costs and how much their absence leaves a hole in our hearts.

We do look at her latest designs in sinh, and we "oooh and ahhh" about the quality craftsmanship, but we don't buy anything (although Malaithong did). Our business targets tomasat textiles. But we do collect smiles and handshakes on the way out, and we promise to drop by next time we're in town.

CHAPTER TWENTY-NINE

# Cotton Textiles

While silk gets a lot of celebrity attention, cotton is the traditional workhorse of practical cloth-making throughout Laos; in fact, it is the world's most commonly-used natural fiber, comprising 39 percent of all textiles made (synthetics have a 58 percent share).

Today, there is less cotton processing in Xam Tai than has been traditional; silk's local tradition and its international allure provide a modern economic opportunity for the regional weavers who wish to earn money. Cotton, on the other hand, carries little economic shimmer; it is a common fiber processed by most all Lao ethnic groups (at least before the modern era of factory-made clothing). In our travels in northwest and central Laos, and especially in Luang Nam Tha and Luang Prabang Provinces, we find considerably more cotton farming and weaving.

Noh, in Na Sala, is spinning cotton on her hand-cranked spindle wheel.

Three or four generations ago, the vast majority of men and women in Xam Tai and Meung Kuan Districts did wear locally-woven, indigo-dyed cotton clothing. Cotton grows easily, works well in both cooler and hotter weather, is durable and easy to wash, and takes indigo dye very well. Combining a warp of cotton and a weft of silk in cloth-making is not uncommon, as this adds strength and warmth to a fabric, but it also adds considerable cost (be it labor, barter, or cash).

In 2016, most villagers in the region are wearing factory-made clothing (except for the women's sinh) and most of these western-fashioned shirts, pants, and underclothing are synthetic or a poly-cotton blend. As mentioned before, the majority of people, and especially those who live in more isolated villages (and who are thus less tied to modern market economies), wear western-made clothing that has been rejected by the western market. From a villager's economic standpoint, the time and effort to manufacture locally-raised cotton clothing is just not practical. Local markets in every moderate-sized village sell new western-style clothing as well, right next to the skeins of cotton-blend and acrylic factory-spun yarns that allow home weavers to bypass the cotton production process, save for the final step of actually weaving.

That said, there are still traditional households which plant, harvest, process, and weave cotton solely for their families' own use. And, thanks to the continued Lao homage of the sinh, there is still a market for both spun yarn and handspun cotton sinh. Mai, profiled on page 206, is weaving cotton for a sinh that will be worn in her family.

Cotton sinh need not be monotone or plain; many have colorful embellishments. A cotton warp and weft can still include discontinuous supplemental pattern wefts of silk. The silk on cotton, in truth, still allows the textile an edge of glimmer and sheen. Many of the sinh you see on the women in the photos are cotton or poly-cotton with silk's added sparkle.

Cotton seeds of the genus *Gossypium* are planted after the summer monsoon has begun, usually in June. While seeds can be obtained from last year's crop, cotton seed is also readily available in the market. Cotton requires little tending and is harvested after six or seven months, when the fluffy cotton seedheads open up and present their white filaments. Lao cotton's maximum staple length is 33 mm, or about 1¼ inch.

In order to learn how locals process cotton, we traveled to the town of Na Sala, about 20 miles (30 km) east of Xam Neua, just beyond the ikat-weaving village of

Left: Noh ginning cotton with a homemade roller gin. Bottom: Bowing cotton to fluff it up. Below right: Making punis (kon) by rolling the bowed cotton around a bamboo rod.

Saleui. Malaithong (who else?) had a good friend named Thong (the "t" is hard, the "h" being an aspirant) whom we had met years earlier and who had supplied us with several sinh-lengths of gorgeous handspun, indigo-dyed cotton. She and her mother, Khom Boun, are lifelong cotton spinners, dyers and weavers.

On our most recent visit, Malaithong had other obligations, so we were joined by another translator from the Xam Neua Tourism Office named Me. Lo and behold, Me's aunt, Noh, also happens to live in tiny Na Sala, and she is also a cotton dyer and weaver. Both Maren and I, even after all these years, still marvel as to how the interconnected flow of relationships always seems to work to everyone's benefit.

The cotton weavers of Na Sala still process cotton the way of their ancestors; no automated machinery or new implements have been developed to speed up the process in family and small village production.

The cotton is hand picked in winter after the essential fall rice harvest is complete and the evenings gain a bit of crispness. Burlap and old rice bags full of the picked cotton's bolls are then dumped onto a tarp or onto a wide flat basket in the front courtyard, and the locks—the fibers within the boll—are picked up by hand and run through a hand-crafted, hand-operated wooden cotton gin (in Lao, *iit*)—a device that squeezes each cotton lock between two rolling pins which thus extract the hard seeds at the core of the fluffy ball.

The now-flattened cotton locks, after being ginned, are then bowed (in Lao, *kong phai*). A wooden bow about four feet (1.2 m) long with a nylon string (and which looks like an archery bow) is dipped into the pile of cotton fiber; then the string is plucked

Sii, a Tai Dam woman, holds her handspun cotton.

as the bow is repeatedly lifted and dipped back into the pile of ginned cotton. The combination of the string's plucking and the bow's thwacking lightens the embrace of the fiber's clingy grip on itself. Essentially, the bowing process introduces more space between the cotton fibers so they can slip past each other as they are spun into thread.

The bowed cotton can now be spun (in Lao, *pan phai*). Holding a cotton puni, or kon, with the left hand, the spinner first hooks the edge of the fiber onto a notch cut into the end of a metal horizontally-aligned spindle. She turns the crank with her right hand, which causes the spindle to rotate very rapidly. She then pulls her left arm back, attenuating the cotton into a thin yarn. The spindle twists the arm's length of yarn as the spinner adjusts her pull, seeking a consistent tension on the fibers between her hand and the spindle; a carefully-moderated pull generates a consistent yarn.

With the left arm extended fully back and a meter-long stretch of newly-spun cotton yarn, the spinner now leans forward, and the yarn detaches from the notch at the end of the spindle. The spun yarn is then wound onto the spindle's shaft.

There is a gentle and quiet rhythm to spinning: the "ka-chikka, ka-chikka" of the wheel's crank, the slow and even backward draw of the left hand, and then the quick return, and the copp of yarn on the spindle's shaft grows a bit more. Another puni of cotton is joined to the loose end of the spun yarn and the process is repeated, and a continuous thread of soft cotton accumulates.

Eventually the shaft is bloated with yarn. The spinner now reaches for the skein winder, which in Houaphan Province comes in two styles. In one style, the spinning wheel itself doubles as a skein winder. The spinner attaches the end of the cotton yarn to the ferris-wheel shaped structure and cranks the wheel in the opposite direction as when spinning. The yarn from the shaft unwinds as the wheel is spun, and is reassembled in larger loops of cotton about three feet (1 m) in circumference, a manageable-sized skein of yarn, for dyeing and weaving. Another style of skein winder is a separate hand-crafted, hand-cranked four-armed contraption that also quickly rewinds the yarn into convenient skeins.

While some cotton is bleached (by boiling in lye) and woven into white cotton cloth, most cotton in Na Sala, once wound into skeins, is destined for the indigo dye vat to create the deep blue cloth for traditional daily-wear cottons and matmi sinh.

Sii's cotton is dyed with maak bao, the root of a jungle vine. She weighs her skeins with a hand-held scale to determine the sale price.

# CHAPTER THIRTY

# Dyeing with Indigo

Once the cotton is spun into skeins, most of it will be dyed in indigo to a deep blue, the color of almost all traditional daily-wear clothing, and still the staple color of women's cotton sinh.

In Houaphan Province, indigo is extracted from the leaves of the plant *Strobilanthes flaccidifolius* (in Lao, *hohm*). The plant grows naturally in the jungle, but it is also cultivated. Noh has planted a hedge of it bordering a rice field behind her home, and thus conveniently harvests the leaves about ten steps from her dye vat.

To get the dye to adhere to the cotton or silk fiber, the leaf extraction must be soaked in a strong alkaline solution to which a sugar is added. The sugar activates the vat's bacteria which, in turn, extracts the oxygen from the mixture, permitting the dye to adhere to the fiber. While indigo dye adheres well to cotton and silk, alkaline solutions do weaken silk threads. Thus, silk threads dyed in indigo either require the extra step

of rinsing in an acid bath, or the threads have to have an overdye applied (another dye applied on top of the indigo dye); both processes neutralize the alkalinity.

There are three steps to making indigo dye: making an indigo "paste," preparing the dye vat, and dyeing the yarns. The following recipe is courtesy of Thong, Khon Boun, Noh, and Patricia Cheesman.

### Step One: Making Indigo Paste

Collect an armload of fresh leaves—go ahead and fill the pot to the brim—and soak them in water for twenty-four to forty-eight hours. The leaves will cause the water to turn a fairly bright, smelly green as the indican in the leaves is converted into indoxyl in a process called enzymic hydrolysis. Do not let the leaves soak for more than forty-eight hours; if they rot, the dye is ruined.

Remove the soggy leaves and beat slaked lime into the mixture, one handful or so for every ten liters of green liquid. The mixture must be vigorously churned to add oxygen.

Noh obtains slaked lime powder by finding a block of limestone (readily available at road cuts and quarries), heating it in a fire until it is glowing red, and then, using tongs, dropping it into a pot of cool water.

Above: Noh prepares to dye. Right: She pours out the excess liquid on top of the indigo in the dye vat.

The stone shatters to fine bits and powder.

After thirty or so minutes of churning, the oxygenation will turn the liquid through a variety of greens and into blue, and a blue precipitate will start to fall out of the liquid. The bath should get quite frothy.

Let the liquid sit and settle; the blue precipitate will separate and collect on the bottom of the pot, while the liquid will turn from blue to brown. Drain the liquid off. The blue sludge at the bottom of the pot is the good stuff, and at this stage the thick paste can be stored in earthenware until one is ready to prepare the dye vat.

Noh adds lao-lao to the indigo dye pot to "sweeten" it.

## Step Two: Preparing the Dye Vat

Note from Patricia Cheesman: If you are a very traditional weaver, start your dye bath on the rising moon and do not work with indigo when you are menstruating. If you believe a spirit inhabits the dye vat, offerings and prayers may be appropriate.

Mix the indigo paste with lye. To make lye, get a bucket or basket with small holes in the bottom and fill it with ash from burned coconut husks, banana leaves, or rice stalks. Pour water through the ash and collect the lye (alkaline water) as it comes out the holes in the bucket's bottom; its pH will be about 12.

Add a bit of "sweet" to the paste/lye slurry, either lao-lao (rice whiskey) as Noh chooses, or a piece of fresh fruit. This will start a fermentation process. Cheesman notes that some weavers at this point add nails or chilis to the mixture to ward off nefarious spirits.

Stir gently; add more sweet until it looks "just right."

Let sit several days. The dye vat will be ready sooner if the weather is hot and dry; it will take longer in cool, wet weather. The vat will turn from blue back to green as the bacteria in the fermentation process removes the oxygen. The dye bath is now ready to receive skeins of yarn as indigo will only adhere to fibers in this anoxic state.

This fermenting dye vat can be kept "alive" for years by adding indigo paste, lye, and sweet whenever more is needed. Every successful indigo dyer has her methods and secrets to an excellent and perpetual vat of indigo.

## Step Three: Dyeing the Yarns

Important: The dyeing process oxidizes the dye bath. A dyer might want to reserve a full cup of the anoxic (lacking oxygen) liquid before dyeing, as this can act as a "starter" for a depleted indigo dye vat. Allow time between dye sessions so the vat can revive and become anoxic again.

Stir the dye bath gently, trying not to disrupt the sediment on the vat's bottom.

Immerse your water-dampened skeins of cotton in the vat, and squeeze the yarns under the liquid's surface until they are

The result: a rich indigo color on a handspun cotton skein.

fully soaked. Use your hands to squish the skeins: it is an honor in any weaving village to walk around with blue-dyed hands. Soak for five minutes. (If dyeing silk, a longer soak time is necessary.)

Lift the skeins from the vat, and squeeze out the moisture. The skeins will, as if touched by a spirit, turn from green to blue right in front of your eyes as the oxygen from the air oxidizes the dye.

Dry the skeins in the shade.

Repeat to obtain a deeper blue, and repeat again for an even deeper blue. The deepest indigos are achieved with about ten baths.

When you have the desired depth of shade, wash the skeins until the water runs clear and the excess dye on the yarns is fully removed.

Dry once more; the yarn is now ready for the loom.

Deep indigo-dyed materials can be further processed to turn black by boiling the skeins in a dye made from the root maak bao, the shrub leaf ben, or the bark of the kor ben; this process will have the benefit of neutralizing the alkalinity, making it safer for silk.

A weaver's personal basket holds a skein of cotton, bobbins, her shuttle, and, of course, her cell phone.

# Five. Looking Forward

*We sleep, but the loom of life never stops, and the pattern which was weaving when the sun went down is weaving when it comes up in the morning.*

*—Harriet Beecher Stowe*

CHAPTER THIRTY-ONE

# The Marketplace

The last two hundred years, generally speaking, have been tough on the Xam Tai marketplace. The fact that the culture and its arts emerge healthy and creatively in the twenty-first century marketplace speaks to the tenacity, pragmatism, and strength of generations of local leaders and of the people themselves.

The silk and textile marketplace of the region before the nineteenth century has not been detailed. Textiles themselves from earlier centuries rarely survive the ravages of time—a silk or cotton textile's life, even if well-treated and rarely used, does not stretch beyond 200 years unless preserved in a museum-like environment. We do know that the region, from the twelfth through the eighteenth centuries, had many generations when the regional muangs politically and economically cooperated, and we do know that silk and textile creation has played a significant role in the livelihoods of inhabitants for many centuries.

Silk textiles contribute a great deal to Xam Tai's economy. Their variety, beauty, and technical excellence are unsurpassed.

Then the "modern challenges": two hundred years ago, a forced and largely successful depopulation, directed by the Siamese. Two generations later the French enforce colonial rule, and then pay scant attention to rural districts, keeping them isolated, undeveloped and politically powerless. Then a vicious war that grows from a regional power struggle into the fiercest and most lopsided bombing campaign ever waged. Left leveled, but still with pride intact, Xam Tai's people again began to rebuild their homes and lives.

When post-war Laos first cracked open its doors to non-citizen entrepreneurs in the late 1970s, some of the first to arrive were textile collectors and businesspeople, predominately from Thailand, who swooped into remote regions seeking older, valuable silks; after all, it had been two generations since any business dealings had been possible, and the new, modern collector's market was hungry to exploit the opportunity. The cash-poor survivors were easily persuaded to relinquish trunk loads of treasure, not always realizing the international market value and cultural significance of what they sold.

Starting in the 1980s and continuing to emerge step by step into these early decades of the twenty-first century, Laos has continued to develop its tourist and other business infrastructure so more tourists and businesspeople can be more comfortable and confident in more places. Today, this lure and inevitability of economic opportunity and modern technology is creating dynamic changes in the marketplace and creating new pressures on, and opportunities for, the textile creators.

A first reaction might be to divide these changes into "positives" and "negatives," and not so long ago I might have harbored a romantic notion that "traditional ways and arts" practiced by "traditional peoples" should remain static, yet intact. Thankfully, the pragmatic leaders and people of Xam Tai share a confidence that together, as a community, they can engage the economic and other opportunities of modernism without violating the cultural ethics and traditions that have allowed this textile-savvy culture to persevere.

In one long generation, four markets for woven textiles have been established for regional silks. First, there are the tourists that visit Laos, and reaching this audience requires getting textiles to the few locations where tourists congregate, namely the cities of Luang Prabang and Vientiane (secondarily, the southern cities of Pakse and Savannakhet). Laos generally attracts two types of tourists: budget-minded backpack travelers and high-end cultural adventurers. Both groups buy silks, but the first will stay in a $12 room, eat $5 meals, and seek the $20 gift, and the second will stay in a $400 room, order a fine French wine with dinner, and may purchase a masterpiece phaa phi mon for $1200. By the way, the new four- and five-star hotels and boutiques are not only catering to Europeans, Australians, and Americans, but are also welcoming a new, wealthy class of Chinese and other Asian tourists.

Xam Tai's quality, reputation, and tradition squarely appeal to and support this higher-end market. Xam Tai's artists also believe this market will grow, and understand that maintaining the highest quality and standards, including a rigorous adherence to remain tomasat (natural), will support its reputation and luxury appeal. However, these tourists rarely come to Xam Tai, so the textiles must be taken to the markets that they frequent.

The second market is overseas, selling handwoven textiles in boutiques and other culturally-savvy stores usually located in major international cities such as Singapore, Tokyo, and Paris. This market would be more likely filled by a business that is directed by someone with a western-trained aesthetic seeking to use Lao traditional imagery in a shape and design to create apparel for the stylish westerner. As such, most exports of "handwoven Lao textiles" are, in fact, western-tailored clothing that have borrowed certain motifs and design elements found in traditional textiles, but are not, in themselves, traditional textiles designed by the cultural tradition's inheritors. The weavers for these textiles would more likely work regular hours at a company's production facility near an urban center.

There are some traditional weavers who see this as cultural appropriation, and thus inappropriate. However, the designers and exporters we have met are generous to a fault, and while they may alter traditional designs to be more "appropriate" for the western market, they work diligently and fairly to support local weavers and traditions.

The third market is that of the individual textile collector and enthusiast, who nurtures the artistic value and cultural relevance of the artform. These fanatics (yes, Maren and I are members of this club) all have their excuses for why they love and collect cultural art, and many are textile artists and hobbyists themselves who deeply appreciate the skill, beauty, diligence, talent, and tradition on display. This audience tends to be attracted to weaving guilds, fiber arts events, and cultural museums; many have had their own travel adventures in pursuit of cultural exploration. The possibilities of internet shopping will further develop this market.

The fourth emerging market is the developing middle class of Lao citizens, which is probably having the greatest impact of all on changing textile design and use. In our decade of visiting, we have very much seen the impact of this emerging economic force on traditional weaving styles and weavers. For example, from our first visit in 2005 until 2012, tiin sinh, the narrow decorative hem stitched onto the bottom of a traditional skirt, could be readily purchased in Xam Neua's and Xam Tai's marketplace. We ourselves purchased and sold many beautiful tiin sinh, as westerners appreciated them as table runners. However, by 2013, tiin sihn as separate elements had virtually vanished and have been replaced with skirts that have the patterned hem woven directly onto the bottom of an elongated sinh, and not on a separate thin band to be stitched on later.

In the urban Lao markets, the most stunning of these newest "one-piece" creations—if crafted of village-raised, naturally-dyed, hand-reeled silk—may cost hundreds of dollars. It is a new market, and weavers of throughout Laos are eager to fill it. On the downside, the talented traditional weavers who are now designing fashion sinh for Lao's elite are no longer weaving healing clothes (phaa sabai) and shaman's shawls (phaa phi mon) for the less predictable tourist markets.

Further, this emerging Lao market is creating a demand for weaving sinh using synthetic fibers. These sinh are nearly as beautiful, and may require just as much weaving effort, but their cost in the marketplace is a fraction of the silk version, as no sericulture, reeling, or dyeing is needed—plus you can throw them in a washing machine!

Such changes remind us that:

- today's wearers are less concerned that their clothing reflects their personal ethnic identification,
- there is little need and desire for people in Laos to identify others as to their ethnicity,
- there is a growing confidence that a nationalized identity, as a "person of Laos," fulfills both the very human desire to belong as well as the pragmatic desire to thrive in a modern world (in short: less tribalism, more nationalism),
- an effective national education system is ensuring that children of all ethnic

## CAVEAT IN THE MARKETPLACE

"*Mai Lao*?" Maren inquired. "Is this Lao silk?" The cloth felt smooth and rich, but it seemed just too flawless.

"Oh, yes, madam. Excellent quality," the shopkeeper smiled. "The best in Vientiane."

Maren took the edge of the textile and, setting her glasses at the tip of her nose, examined the textile's fringe up close. "It drapes like silk, but…" Maren mumbled to herself.

She pulled out a lighter from the bottom of her shoulder bag and isolated a single thread from the fringe. The vendor furrowed her brow and leaned forward.

The flame touched the thread, which instantly flared and rolled back on itself into a small black ball. Maren rolled the tar-like wad between her thumb and forefinger and put them to her nose; she shared the scent with the shopkeeper. The burnt thread smelled of burnt plastic. The Lao call it "Chinese silk," and the thread was 100% acrylic.

Had the material been silk, the burned filament would have left a small bit of crumbly gray ash that would disappear with a quick finger rub, and it would have smelled lightly of cooked protein. (Had it been cotton, it would have left a long ash and smelled like a burning plant.)

Give the yarn engineers and manufacturers credit—the material shimmered like silk, and its soft drape could fool even the most sensitive skin.

The vendor raised her brow and then frowned; she looked as disappointed as we were. We smiled and nodded. Like many people in the marketplace, she too had been fooled.

groups learn, among other things, the Lao language and Lao history,

• there are, and must continue to be, leaders in the weaving industry and marketplace who can identify, shape, and fulfill the needs of a diverse and growing customer base,

• the nation's people have now reached beyond "subsistence and survival" and have begun to participate in and desire the comfort, convenience, and integrity that comes with modernity.

These changes create new pressures for weavers, as these new markets demand consistency, quality, and an attention to fashion.

These changes also necessitate a pause—a moment to recognize that the momentum of modernity by its very definition challenges the traditional, and that cultural integrity is rooted in nurturing a delicate balance between the sure past and the anticipated future.

These traditional silk artists and communities are rareties. The weavers of Xam Tai and Meung Kuan Districts are some of Laos's, and the world's, last "hold-outs" who live what they do—who maintain the integrity and dynamic of traditional weaving as a lifestyle and essential way of transmitting culture and leading a healthy life. Additionally, this community of independent artists is steering a path that works to ensure that these vital, inherited weaving traditions provide economic stability and respect for the participants and their families.

Xam Tai's mood is optimistic. Just last year, the district vice governor of Xam Tai District, a civil engineer, showed Maren and me a schematic of a park with a pavilion he hopes to have built at the site of the town's old marketplace. The site, he reminded us, is now a vacant block across the street from the new Lao Development Bank. He grinned as he showed us, on an iPhone app he had programmed, the three-dimensional layout he envisioned. It did look impressive.

Local weavers were talking about the attraction and how it would increase tourism, too. Several were imagining a "Xam Tai Weaving Center" near the redevelopment that would showcase local traditions and methods of silk raising, dyeing and weaving. It would also have to be large enough, they reasoned, to host an extensive gift shop.

CHAPTER THIRTY-TWO

# Mai of Meung Kuan

She sits at one of several floor looms that huddle under a traditional stilted home set in the middle of Meung Kuan's redevelopment project. Maren, Malaithong and I, who have been walking up the newly paved street, step carefully between the piles of construction dirt and chunks of concrete and approach her from behind.

"Sabaidee," Maren asks lightly, not wanting to startle her.

The elder stops her hands and turns her head. "Oh, sabaidee-ee," she smiles brightly. Despite the pressing warmth of the late morning sun, she still wears a thick acrylic coat.

She nods several times and then, with her hand, beckons us to come and take a look at what is on the loom. She weaves a colorful tiin sinh—an assertive red, white, gold, and blue twist of silk ngueak set on a black poly-cotton warp and weft. She pulls back the attached supplemental threads and unrolls a forearm's length of the completed piece. She smiles silently as we compliment her work.

Her eyes sparkle. "My name is Mai," she responds through Malaithong, "and I am eighty-eight years old." She seems proud of her age.

"I learned to weave when I was eight or nine years old," she continues. "When I was young I wove mostly cotton, for sinh. But I also learned to reel and weave silk. I married young and had eight children, four sons and four daughters, and seven of them are alive today. Two of my children live here in Meung Kuan, but I also have three children in Xam Tai and two in Vientiane."

We ask her opinion on all the construction in Meung Kuan.

"This construction is very good," she says. "The recent changes are very good for us. We now have electricity, and the new road makes it easier to go to other places. It is very easy to have my family visit, and it is also good that my children and grandchildren can travel to see other places."

She looked straight into my eyes. "When I was young, life was very poor. We had to work very hard every day just to get food. We always worried we might not have enough."

"Now that things are modern, we can just go to the market. There is food there every day. I can even buy my silk thread for weaving in the market," she admits, and then she pauses a moment. "Today it is so easy to go places and see different things."

We ask if she had any good memories from childhood, but she shakes her head. "All I remember is the work."

Did you teach your children to weave?

"All of my daughters are weavers, and I have eleven granddaughters, and they all weave as well. I am very proud of them." She pauses, and then blushes a girlish smile.

"I wish I were fourteen years old again," she suddenly confesses with a toothy grin and a fling of her hands. "There is now so much to look forward to—so many places to go. It is a good time to be young!"

Above: Mai cheerily chats about her town. Opposite: Mai weaves a tiin sinh on her loom under the porch.

CHAPTER THIRTY-THREE

# The Dance of the Young Weavers

Our first few days in Xam Tai had been a social flurry as we re-connected with our weaving friends and business contacts. The two American friends who were visiting with us, both seasoned travelers and textile enthusiasts, seemed genuinely surprised at the hospitality, artistry, and vibrancy of the community, and Souksakone, Phout, Lun, Bounkeo, Sukkhavit, Tiip and others had been welcoming and generous with their energy and time. Even the shopkeeper who sells Beer Lao on the corner welcomed us with a smiling "Sabaidee-ee" and handshakes—and a reminder, as had been a joke the previous year, to buy a large bag of *nam kohn*—ice.

The wedding couple shares a solemn moment of dance.

March, because it is a time of little fieldwork, is the wedding season, and on our day of arrival each of us had received pink-hearted invitations. Malaithong translated that we had been invited to attend the wedding of the son of the governor of Meung Kuan District, which was to be held here in Xam Tai. What an honor!

At dusk on the auspicious day, we dressed in our best clothes, each woman donning a locally-woven silk phaa phai and sinh, and walked to the open-air public pavilion next to the market, where a fleet of tables and hundreds of plastic chairs had been set. Several hundred walkers and motorcycles, some ferrying families of four, arrived within fifteen minutes of each other, and the chattering crowd quickly filled the venue.

Souksakone, Hamman, Phout, Malaithong, and the four of us falang were escorted by a cheerful usher with a red boutonniere to a central table. In the middle of the table stood three bottles of Beer Lao (with more in a yellow case behind Hamman's chair), and bottles of orange Fanta, 7Up, and water. Dinner was already on the table, each serving dish covered in plastic wrap: local fried sausage and tripe, traditional Lao *laap* (minced pork with banana flower), steamed greens, a large bowl of water buffalo soup with carrots and meat, and individually wrapped banana leaves filled with glutinous sticky rice. Souksakone opened a Beer Lao and started pouring glassfuls for everyone.

A minute later a wide-eyed groom and his silk-bedecked bride arrived at our tableside. Phout said something that included a very long vowel-tone and both the groom and bride shared wide smiles. The bride held a tray upon which sat two short glasses and the groom presented a bottle of Johnny Walker Black; each of us was offered, in turn, a taste of the elixir and a moment of acknowledgement with the young couple.

Now we could eat, and we filled our individual plates and bowls with the community-made fare, and then we filled our plates again. The beer and soda flowed.

The master of ceremonies turned up the volume, offered some bubbly words, and then began to sing a slow traditional melody. The wedding couple, along with their two sets of parents, joined each other in the open area and began to dance. A few minutes later, more couples joined. The paired dancers stood side by side and slowly walked the perimeter of the dance area. The steps were short and taken with a dip in the knee, and the hands of each person, with fingers stretched outward, moved in a wave-like pattern at waist level—first to the left, then to the right—as seen in Thai

Everyone joins in for *lamvong* (traditional Lao dancing). Note the beautiful assortment of sinh.

and Khmer dancing. More couples joined the growing circle of dancers; at first, most pairs appeared to be married couples, but soon there were also women dancing with women and men with men, and several adults joined with children. The dancers were smiling, but, like the music, their energy was tempered and formal. The song lasted perhaps five minutes.

The next song reintroduced the drum machine and suddenly a loud, cheerful pop tune erupted, setting off a sharp crackle in the speakers. The rhythm picked up, and some of the dancers became more expressive with their arm and dip motions. Yet the dance remained essentially the same: small dipping steps forward, side by side with a dance partner in a single, communal circle made as wide as needed to include all participants. Every thirty steps or so, at a cue from the master of ceremonies, each couple would face each other, raise their right hands, and do a promenade around the other, returning to their original position.

Phout stood up and held out her hand to Maren, and the two joined the dance; Malaithong invited our friend Joe, Hamman invited Linda, and then Souksakone looked at me with raised eyebrows. We joined the circle and shared smiles for two up-beat pop songs and then returned to our table, where Hamman poured another round of beer. The music was quite loud and we had to almost shout to be heard across the table.

I was leaning back in my chair, caught up in the cheer and the chatter and the colors, when I felt a double tap on my right shoulder. I turned in my chair and faced a young woman. I recognized her as having been one of the school-age weavers who had, earlier that day, showed us her handwoven work at Phout's home—she is perhaps eleven or twelve years old. She had come to our table with two of her friends, also young weavers, who had tapped on Maren's and Joe's shoulders.

The young ladies were requesting a dance.

We all joined the circle, and, as is traditional, turned toward our partners and pressed our hands together in a formal sabaidee and bowed slightly. The music started, another sanguine pop song, and we turned and started to dance side by side in the wide circle. I moved my hands back and forth, and with each small step forward I bent my knees to the music's rhythm.

I glanced at my partner out of the corner of my eye. She arched her hands gracefully and smoothly to the left, then to the right; each slight dip with the knee was measured and precise. Her movements were practiced; her intent eyes focused forward. I followed her lead, straightening my back, and focused on smoothing the flow of my arms' motions, and feeling the weight of each dip with my legs. This dance surely felt more formal and serious than my previous turns on the dance floor, and I concentrated on embracing the music and the movement with the same poise and solemnity of my dance partner.

The forwardness and seriousness of the young weavers who had invited us to join the dance was admirable and revealing. These were the young women, no doubt, who would soon be assuming the challenges and responsibilities of steering the community's art and ethic, balancing the act of upholding tradition and engaging new opportunity. This leadership surely requires courage, and I smiled to myself with renewed confidence that the community would indeed find competent, strong leadership in the next generation.

Together, with dozens of other celebrants, we danced, acknowledging the new couple and the specialness of the evening. Together, we celebrated our camaraderie and destiny as we embraced the ways of the ancestors and the promise of the future.

The young weaver led our formal dance

three times around the circle until the music stopped and the master of ceremonies charged into cheerful words I could not understand. My dance partner and I turned toward each other, nodded with our hands clasped under our chins, and returned to our respective tables.

Maren and Joe joined me back at the table with the others "That was sweet!" Maren exclaimed. "What a graceful young woman," Joe commented. I said that I had been forced to refine my casual dancing style, and everyone laughed.

Souksakone smiled and opened another beer. Hamman raised his refilled glass and we all met his eyes. He lifted his chin a touch and spoke a sentence, then looked at Malaithong. She translated: "Hamman says that he is, tonight, happy not just for the wedding couple, but he is also happy that all of us are here and could join in celebration." She paused as Hamman spoke another sentence. "He says that he is thankful for the friendship and business of his falang friends, and he has very big wishes that we will spend many more evenings together."

Hamman looked surely at each of us while Malaithong translated, and then he added one more sentence and nodded. Malaithong smiled. "Hamman says…uh, how do I say… he says that we are more when we are together. That celebrating and working together is for our good health, for always."

We all looked into our friends' eyes and smiled, then raised our glasses to our lips, and the sound of the celebration poured over us, rolling out over the town, and across the fields, and up into the dark and ageless hills.

The newly-married couple greets each guest with a personal toast.

CHAPTER THIRTY-FOUR

# Mai Chom of Xam Tai

We formally met Mai Chom in 2014, when she was eight years old. We were in Phout's home, and perhaps twenty-five of Xam Tai's weavers, each with a few textiles to share, sat on the floor in a semicircle around Maren and me. Phout had recommended that we first look at the textiles of the pre-adolescent weavers, eight of whom were present, because they had to return soon to school for the afternoon sessions. They came forward and sat patiently on their knees with their "love tokens" and other silks in their laps, each waiting a turn to present her work.

Maren asked the name of each girl in turn and examined every textile, making sure every young weaver was praised for her effort and product. As usual, we purchased at least one textile from each, handing the appropriate cash to each child for her work. (Prices had been pre-set by the adult weavers.)

One young weaver, an eight-year-old who was contributing for her first time, seemed almost to tremble as she handed her few pieces to Maren. Having your work examined and critiqued in front of your mother and much of the village by "the Americans" requires courage.

Maren smiled and picked up the first "love token" the young weaver had presented. She squinted carefully at the textile's design, and her smile dropped. She picked up the next, stretched it between her hands, and pulled it close to her eyes. Maren peered over the top of her glasses at the young woman.

"Did you weave these yourself?" Maren inquired through Malaithong. The girl stiffened, and then turned to look at her mom in the back, and then turned back to Maren.

"*Chou*," she mouthed—her breath was so light. Maren turned her eyes to the third small silk. Sometimes an older weaver will try to sneak a textile into a girl's stack, perhaps in an effort to sell it or perhaps in an effort to elevate a daughter's status in front of everyone.

Maren double-checked, her eyes glancing from textiles to the girl's eyes: "You did all the weaving…?" Malaithong didn't translate.

"*Chou*," the girl said again, this time in an audible whisper. Her doe eyes stared at Maren, waiting for the comments. Behind the girl, her mother nodded confirmation to Maren as well that the girl was indeed the artist.

Maren handed me one of the tokens. The motifs were sharp and tight—every thread held its proper place. Not a single supplemental color spot seemed misplaced. Not a single blemish indicated the work of a novice.

And that is how we met Mai Chom.

She had started weaving at age seven, and her parents, Intong and Nang Phei, who have four older sons but no other daughters, quickly realized that she had not merely a talent for weaving, but a gift.

Now, at age ten, she is weaving full phaa biang, and, at our sales, her work sits alongside the other adult weavers' work. Her patience, her precision, her dexterity—they are as mature and confident as any of the master weavers in Xam Tai.

Mai Chom does well in school, and enjoys her environmental studies class the most. She does find two or three hours a day to weave at her loom that sits in an open shed structure next to the family's small tractor, a few steps from the front door.

She nods when asked if she likes to weave, and her expression and demeanor as she concentrates on her work is intent. Her hands move in a perfect rhythm with the loom's mechanics. She says it now only takes her about twenty days to complete a narrow, two-meter-long phaa biang, a pace consistent with experienced weavers.

She dreams of becoming a doctor, and pink is her favorite color.

Below: Mai Chom weaving a phaa sabai. Right: The strong face of the future of Xam Tai.

EPILOGUE

# The Final Word

Sukkhavit holds out the iridescent phaa phi mon textile in her hands—a pattern and color completely different than any we had seen during our entire week in Xam Tai.

"Sukkhavit," we say through Malaithong. "We really can afford no more." And, in truth, our budget for this visit is long shot. We have enough Lao funds just to get the two of us on the sixteen-hour busride to Hanoi, which would be leaving in an hour, but no more. Our Lao kip and U.S. cash were spent, and any upcoming Vietnam expenses prior to our arrival in Hanoi could only be drawn from our modest reserve of Vietnamese dong.

Sukkhavit's eyes grow moist; she looks at the ground.

"I am so poor," she says. "If I could only sell this one more, it would be so helpful."

We re-explain the financial situation we had spoken about yesterday and remind her that we had made many purchases of her things over the last several days.

She shakes her head.

"I have children to feed," she continues, her lower lip just short of a tremble. "I have a son in college, and it is very expensive."

We nod in empathy. Sukkhavit pushes the textile up to Maren's eyes. It is one we had not seen, and, well—no doubt—it is absolutely beautiful. And daring.

A perfect and unique blend of rich green, opulent gold, and deep red, with a flawless, precise ngueak motif that dances in a sea of shimmering brown and blue. It is exquisite, on par with the very finest pieces we have seen all week. (You can see it on page 25.)

And we know Sukkhavit knows it, too.

Sukkhavit's voice cracks a little. "I have so little," she continues. "Just this one small piece will help." She now looks so old and bent. Maren and I glance at each other; even Malaithong looks glum.

"*Bo, bo*." I say with a forced laugh. "No, no. Sukkhavit, no more Lao kip," and I turn my front pockets inside out and raise my palm to the sky to show that nothing is left. "*Bo kip. Bo kip.*"

Sukkhavit looks at me, and holds out the silk scarf. She turns her face to Maren with basset-hound eyes and blinks as if she does not understand. Maren and I freeze. Malaithong's voice slows and deepens a little, just like Sukkhavit's, and the tones flatten. "I am so poor, and I have so little."

Sukkhavit pushes her hand into her cotton purse and two fingers emerge like blind snakes through the bottom. "Look—the mice have been eating my bag. And I cannot afford a new one."

And she poses there, on the side of the road, two of her gnarled fingers sticking out of the bottom of the cheap, commercial purse, a few strands of graying hair drifting in front of her face.

Maren and Sukkhavit lock eyes. Maren raises her eyebrows and gives Sukkhavit a goofy "you've-got-to-be-kidding" look. Sukkhavit's deep pout flutters, and then slowly her lips rise into a grin, and then a wide smile. She laughs and grabs Maren by the left shoulder with her right arm, sharing the joke. With her left hand, she brings the textile again in our direction, nodding. Not really pleading, but more knowing. The textile really is a stunner.

Maren's determined look fades, and she and Sukkhavit lean into each other, wrapping their arms around each other's waist. Sukkhavit cackles, and her now stronger voice throws out a few untranslated lines, and we all laugh.

Three minutes later, we learn that Sukkhavit accepts Vietnamese dong—at a fair exchange rate, of course.

*Falang*, definition 13
Fashion, daily **96**
*Feum* 169ff.
Findly, Ellison 90, 94, 111, 127, 128, 135, 183
Floor loom, traditional Lao 168ff., **171**
France, involvement in Laos 54
Fresh indigo dyeing process 166-167

Giant spirit motif 134
Goddess, Mara 130
Green dye from fresh indigo 166-167, **166-167**

*Haem*, for dyeing yellow 166
Hak, daughter of Souksakone 152
Hamman, husband of Souksakone 118,162
Hanoi, Vietnam 42
Healing cloth **112**, 113
Hintang Archaeological Site 51
Hirschstein, Ari 7, 8, 16, **21**, 29, **30**, **38**, 65, 92-93
Hirschstein, Josh **30**, **33**, **139**, **140**, **141**
Hirschstein, Zall 7, 8, 13, 16, **19**, **21**, 29, **30**, **38**, 65, 139
History, political 51ff.
Hmong 20, 21, 34, 45, 74
Ho Chi Minh Trail 56
*Hohm*, see also indigo 164
*Hong* 111
*Hong/saang* motif, see also bird/elephant 129, 132
Houaphan Province 9, **32**, 36, 42ff., 54
Houaphan Province, ethnic types **68**
*Huea hong* motif, see also hong boat **132**, 133

*Iit*, see cotton gin
Indigo, dyeing cotton with **196**, 197ff.
Indigo, dyeing process 164
Indigo, fresh for dyeing green 166-167
Indigo, from *Strobilanthes flaccidifolius* 164
Indigo, history of 164

Janzen, John M. 87

Kaen, musical instrument **94**
Kaiphet 9, 13, **16**, 36, 92
Kathmandu, Nepal 29
Khamanee, husband of Maikhom 123
Khamkong, son of Souksakone 152
*Khang*, see also stick lac 162
*Khao nyeung* 82, 152, 169ff., **170**, **171**, **184**, see also pattern template
*Khit*, see continuous supplemental weft
Khmu Ou ethnic group 70
Khom Boun (Na Sala) **97**, **194**
*Khon buhaan* motif, see also ancestor spirit 129, **130**, **132**, 133, 134
Koh Chang, Thailand 28
*Kong phai*, see cotton bow
*Kor Ben* for dyeing golden brown 165

Lac 76
Lac dyeing process **157-159**
*Lamvong*, see dancing, traditional Lao
Lan Xang Kingdom 53
Lao Cai Province, Vietnam 30
Lao Development Bank 22
Lao food 18, 38, **39**
Lao hai 120
Lao Loum 24, 27, 44, 45, 52, 62, 69, 70-71, 74
Lao-lao 19
Lao-lao, as indigo dye assist 198
Lao-Tai language family 71
Legends, traditional 131
Love tokens 59
Luang Prabang 27, 52, 57
Lun **36**, 39, 77ff., **77**, 78, 122, 154, 160
Lun, textile by **77**, **187**
Lundberg, Kristin Vivian 87, 89

*Maak bao* for dyeing 165, **195**
Mahayana Buddhism 94
Mai (Meung Kuan) 206-207, **207**
Mai (Xam Tai) 66-67, **66 67**
Mai Chom (Xam Tai) 157, **174**, **175**, 212-213, **212-213**
Mai Fong and the Pretty Girl story 131
Maikhom (Xam Tai), mother of Phout 121, **121**
Malaithong **33**, 37, 58, 64, 76, 82, 99, 106, 118, **121**, 137, 150
Man/woman healing cloth 112, 113, **113**, 122
Mango tree bark for dyeing yellow 166
Map **43**
*Marsdenia tinctoria* for green dye 166
*Matmi*, see weft ikat weaving
Matrilineal structure of Lao Loum 64
Me Tau Hom, shaman skirt of **117**
Me Tau Lu 88
Me Tau Lu (Ban Tao) 82-84, **83**, **84**, **85**
Mekong Basin 55
Mekong Delta, Vietnam 30
Mekong River 52
Memory sticks 183
Meung Kuan District 44
Missionaries, Catholic 54
Moon pattern **115**
*Mophone* 95, 123
Mordant, *Acacia rugata* 163
Mosquito-net border **104**, 104
Motifs 127ff.
  baby neuk with scales **128**
  box of naga 46, **58**
  crab **84**
  *naga* 130
  *ngueak/naak* 91, 129
  *ngueak*, two headed and single headed, laying eggs **128**
  *phii nyak* 91, **103**, 106, 109, 129, **134**, see also giant spirit
  *siho* 91
  real world 134-135, **135**
  wax naga boat **132**

Muang Et District 74
Muang Phuan 53

Muang Vaen 36, 92
*Muk*, see Supplemental warp weaving
Mulberry **143**

Na Meo 44
Na Sala, cotton spinning in 193
Na Sala, *matmi* weaving in 180
Naga, see naak 130
Nakham 92
Nam Noen 36
Nam Xam river **27**, 44, **48**, **62**, **71**
Nam Xam Wilderness Area 36
Nang Tiip (Xam Tai) 46ff., **46**, **47**, **120**
Nanthavongdouangsy, Viengkham 100, 101, 131
Natural dyeing 159ff.
Nau Tong, husband of Chola 190
Nepal, Kathmandu 27
Net mending **48**
Ngueak/naak, see also river serpent 129
Ni Mon **150**, 151
Noh, indigo dyer **192**, 193ff., **197-198**

Orange dye 167
Oregon, Eugene 29

Paivan, daughter of Chola 190
Pathet Lao 44, 54, 55, 57
Pattern templates, see also *khao nyeung* 82
Pelavong, Phanla 92-93
Petanque 38, **141**
*Phaa Biang* 49, 58, 59, 76, 106
*Phaa haat aeo* see also shaman's belt 115, 218
*Phaa hom*, see blanket, sleeping
*Phaa kan mon*, see also love tokens 59
*Phaa kang*, see door curtain
*Phaa phai*, see also shoulder cloth 115
*Phaa phi mon* **36**, 113, see also shaman's shawl
*Phaa sabai*, see also healing cloth 14, 15, 113
*Phaa tuum* **103**, see blanket, shoulder wrap
Phakhouane 92
Phongsali Province 55
Phonsavan 44
Phonsavan 57
Phouang, daughter of Phout 122
Phouey **116**
Phout **15**, **18**, 27, 33, 38, 39, 100, **112**, 118ff., **118**, **119**, **120**, **121**, 138, 152, **157**, 160
Plain of Jars 51, 52, **52**, **53**, **56**, 57
Plain weave 169ff.
Pliny the Elder 144
*Poei*, see mosquito-net border
Political history 51ff.
Pre-mordanting silk for dyeing 161
Purple dye 167

Red dye 161
Red dye from teak leaves 162
Red Tai, see Tai Daeng 52
Reeling silk **147**
Rice fields **50**
River serpent motif, 111, 129, see also ngueak/naak

*Saang hong* 130
Saleui 92, 96, 100
Saleui, *matmi* weaving in 180
Sappan 162
Schliesinger, Joachim 69
School uniforms **72**
Sericin 144, 149, 161
Sericulture 137ff., **144**
Seuk (Ban Tao) 145ff., **147**, **148**
Seuk, daughters of **90**
Shaman cloth **110**, 111, **114**
Shaman skirt and headdress **116**
Shaman's belt 115
Shaman's shawls 113
Shamanic healing 111
Shamanic rituals 52, 74
Shamanism 95, 112
Shoulder cloth **115**
*Siho*, see also elephant-lion 16
*Sii* 191
*Sii falang*, see Color for foreigners 112
*sii tomasat*, see also natural color 16
Silk fiber, description of 144
Silk market, history of 203
Silk reeling **147**
Silk textiles, qualities of 35ff.
Silk, grades of 145
Silk, preparing for dyeing 158ff.
Silkworm cocoon fringe **112**, 113
Silkworm cocoons **145**
Silkworm eggs **144**
Silkworm larvae **145**
Silkworm moths **142**
Silkworm pupae 39, 149
Silkworms **138**
*Sinh* 22, 96ff., **96**, **99**, **100**
*Sinh* 96ff.
*Sinh and Lao Women* 100
Sisavangvong, King 54
Souksakone 22, 39, **100**, **118**, **121**, 159ff., **153**, 155, **157**, **158**, **164**, 180ff.
Souksakone, guest house of **63**
Souksakone's grandmother's textile **129**
*Spirits in the Loom* 95
Stowe, Harriet Beecher 200
*Strobilanthes flaccidifolius*, see also indigo 164
Sukkhavit **17**, **19**, **20**, 22ff., **23**, **24**, 36, 37, 46, **214**, 215
Sukkhavit, textile by **25**, **26**
Summer Institute of Linguistics 69
Supplemental stripes 64
Supplemental warp weaving 179
Supplementary pattern warps **178**
Synthetic fibers 36, 102, 204
*Symplocos racemosa* as a mordant 163

Ta (Meung Kuan) 106-109, **107**
Tai Daeng 27, 45, 52, 53, 54, 69, 74, 127
Tai Dam 24, 27, 45, **88**
Tai Lue, tapestry weaving of 157

Tapestry technique 113, **108**, 179-180
Template makers 180ff.
Temple cloth, see also shoulder cloth 114
Textile managers 154-155
Thailand, Bangkok 30, 52
Thailand, Koh Chang 30
That Foun **52**
*The People of Laos: Rural and Ethnic Diversities* 69
Theravada Buddhism 52, 74, 94
*Tiin sinh*, see also skirt borders 22, 85, 98, 102, 191, 204
Tonle Sap, Cambodia 30
Traditional Hilltribe Art 33
Traditional home, description of 44
Turmeric, climbing 165

Unweaving old textile **190**

Van Esterik 101
Vieng Xai 44, 55
Vientiane 32, 55, 57
Vietnam, Hanoi 44
Vietnam, Lao Cai Province 30
Vietnam, Mekong Delta 30

Wallman, Sandra 87
War see also American War 22, 27, 42, 52, 56, 101, 122, 183
War, Vietnamese see also American War 52, 54,
Warping the loom, process 170
Wat Phia Wat **53**
Weaving and economic well-being 87-88
Weaving and social well-being 87-88
Weaving as transmission of culture 90-91
*Weaving Cloth, Weaving Nagas* 131-132
Weaving Shuttle of the King's Daughter story 131
Weaving terms, vocabulary of 172
Wedding, traditional Lao 208-212
Weft ikat 180-181, **181**
Wilderness Area, Nam Xam 44
World Heritage Site, Louang Prabang 57

Xam Neua 36, 38, 42, **45**, 57
Xam Tai **8**, **9**, **28**, **49**, 92
Xam Tai District 42ff., 56
Xam Tai Regional Women's Weaving Cooperative 92
Xam Tai valley **75**
Xam Tai, cultural roots of 69ff.
Xam Tai, progress in 61ff.
Xieng Khouang Province 44, 56, 57
Xiengthongst, son of Souksakone 152

Yangtze River basin 69
*Yiap Koh*, see tapestry-style weaving
Yiim (Xam Tai) 58-59, **58**